Wisdom Kwati

Money Rule

AF790324

Wisdom Kwati

Money Rule

JustFiction Edition

Imprint

Cover image: www.ingimage.com

Publisher:
JustFiction! Edition
is a trademark of
Dodo Books Indian Ocean Ltd., member of the OmniScriptum S.R.L Publishing group
str. A.Russo 15, of. 61, Chisinau-2068, Republic of Moldova Europe
Printed at: see last page
ISBN: 978-620-3-57746-4

MONEY RULE

MONEY RULE

WISDOM KWATI

Email: books@wisdomkwati.com

This book contains fictitious analogies. All identification terms; names, places, and events are purely used on account of the author's imaginative prowess. Resemblance to persons living or dead is outrightly declared coincidental.

Book Project Consultancy/Editing:

Dicta Concepts and Consultation Firm

www.okoyeijeoma.com

For general information about the author and other products or services by the author, visit https://wisdomkwati.com

Wisdom Kwati™

Money Rule/ Wisdom Kwati

Includes index

ISBN: **9786203577464**

PREFACE

Dear reader of Money Rule,
For over 10 years now, I have researched, applied, and have taught thousands of people through my book, eBooks, online platforms, and speaking engagements how to achieve self-development and financial freedom. Now, it's your turn.

In these pages, I'm going to teach you practical formulae to earn more money and secure financial freedom. These are not just ordinary streams of strategies. You will understand the rules of money and will learn how to create the kind of residual income streams that flow into your life even while you sleep.

In addition, I will show you how to gain control of your finances, earn high rates of return – using little-known financial strategies; some even guaranteed by the government.

What will all this get for you? A lifestyle that gives you the freedom to do what you want, when you want, with whomever you want. If this is what you want, let's work together to make it happen in your life.

Prosperously,
your money mentor,
Wisdom Kwati

ACKNOWLEDGEMENTS

Having good people on your team is an important part of becoming a great and successful entrepreneur, and I've been blessed to have some exceptionally great teammates on this project. Zara Shenew deserves special thanks for her unselfish commitment of time, ideas, and energy to this book.

H.E Mrs Grace Chamah; thank you so much for all your encouragement, support and motherly love and advice on this entrepreneurial journey. My sincere appreciation to my team at Karabow Group of Companies. You all have been resourceful in ways and I really do appreciate.

Special thanks to our editorial team at Dicta Concepts and Consultation Firm for not giving up on this book, and for helping me make *Money Rule* a practical, helpful, and inspirational read.

Most of all, I thank the Good Lord for loving me, and for teaching me everything I know about the rules of money. You make my dreams come true every day.

REVIEWS/ENDORSEMENTS

I have gone through the pages of this book and I think it is very different from other books that I have come across. It holds a great diversification from the history of money to financial advice and financial intelligence coupled with an interesting story. I'm impressed because you didn't have to follow the old ways of doing things. I am sure other writers would soon copy your style. Nice book. Well-done!

~ Mr Wale Adewunmi.

CEO, Akkoglobal Tech, Nigeria

In recent times, I have read many articles on 'How to Grow Wealth' especially in an environment like Nigeria and in general, Africa. It is very baffling to know that most 'money-making information' out there are outdated. Little wonder why poverty is still a mass plaque. Today's money market is built on principles, working in synergy with where value is most needed. But how do you find the gold?

Wisdom Kwati, in this book, has made mining money easier and heck! You don't need an academic backup for it. In fact, I can guarantee you that the quality of information here will beat your IMAGINATION and get your mind working.

~ Sharon Pwavi Babele

Cultural Diplomat and Business Lover

If you really want to up your money game and create wealth and riches, you need to know the principles that make people rich and this book contains those principles. Making money is not magic. This book demystifies how money works and it shows you how you can go from where you are financially to creating abundance that your soul desires.

Get a copy for everyone that matters in your life – family, friends, spouse, colleagues, and employees – and together, you can create the prosperity that is within the reach of those who have mastered the rules of money.

~ Usoko Lindam

CEO, Mentor Box

TABLE OF CONTENTS

INTRODUCTION

Whenever the thought of the word 'money' flashes the human mind, certain things come to view. Money is an everyday term hence, everyone thinks money. A good number of hours that constitute a day are often spent on the thought of making or spending money. Human beings are eager to make money. They want to ensure their financial freedom and create no room for lack. They believe that they can make money and that can solve their problem as long as they live. They want to experience this feeling of having enough. This makes them cherish the subject 'Money'.

However, among the very set of people who thinks money, only but a few makes money. While others wish they have all the opportunities to make money, others are held by their limited mindset towards the subject. This makes the perception that "money is meant for a particular class of people" true.

That notwithstanding, a good number of persons are still committed towards this cause. They are ready to change the narratives. They are set to tap the opportunities that lay untouched and become multi-millionaires within the blink of the eyelids. This is exciting.

Whenever the issue of money is brought up, the 21st-century man is, however, at will to accept changing norms or go by outdated systems. The refusal of the new ways of maximizing opportunities to make wealth is what has caused a lot of people go into financial crisis. Applying outdated system to the process of earning more will not only cause you a great loss, but will also get you into struggling while the smart ones achieve huge financial feats.

The rule for making money is no more out of reach. At your doorstep, you can get access to adequate strategies and systems to make more money and play a bigger game. Becoming financially free is easy to achieve with the advent of Internet and high-level technology. These expose us to the rules to achieve financial freedom.

A good number of people are passing through financial crisis because they do not have the knowledge of the rules that govern money. Most people want to hold firm unto their finances but they fail at certain points. The problem, however, is not the lack of desire but the lack of knowledge of how money works.

The inability to get your financial life stable has cost a lot of entrepreneurs their freedom of choice. They cannot take financial decisions due to their financial state. This is why a young man might come up with a great business plan but do not have adequate knowledge of money rules to hold him through earning and spending.

Playing a bigger game in your financial state has never been this easier. The secret to make more money and ensure financial freedom is encapsulated in this book. Building profitable influence and income streams have never been this easier either. Gone are the days when one has to toil day and night to make ends meet. Today, there are smart ways to do that.

For you to achieve total financial freedom, your mind has to be rightly positioned. Apt knowledge of financial systems and models is also needed. You also need to master how to build a steady stream of income. Remember, money fleets.

Bear in mind that your overall success in the issue of finance is dependent on your view of money. I want you to see money from the smart entrepreneur's view instead of what it used to be seen as few years ago. Be updated!

Wisdom Kwati
2020

PHASE 1: MAN AND MONEY

CHAPTER 1

WHAT CONNECTS MAN AND MONEY?

Jane walked into the room after giving the security man at the gate a stern warning not to allow anyone into her house. She had tiredness written all over her face. Her footsteps while returning from the kitchen showed that she might fall to the ground anytime soon. She quickly found herself to a sofa and sighed as though all her burden had rested on it. She panicked as she remembered the day's event. Her head has been filled with thoughts that she felt numb and weak. She stared at the clock. It was 7:30 pm.

Earlier that afternoon, her bank account officer had sent her a mail that the company's account was running red. She couldn't find words to reply the mail. She was going to visit the bank first thing the next morning before heading to the office. Should she talk about the huge financial debt her company owed? She just couldn't understand how all she has been working for was going down the drain in a twinkle of an eyelid. She was tired of her money situation. She didn't even know how she was going to keep at the fact that she had needs to meet.

Among the confusing issues confronting man, money has taken the forefront. The way it grabs the mind of humans each time it is mentioned keeps one wondering what unseen powers it holds. It is not wrong to say that every individual grips at the thought of money. There is this unseen force that throws one into oblivion at its thought.

Man and money is connected in various ways. Its origin is often viewed as an innovative one, hence, its relationship with man. Besides, who uses money? Man right?

Money came from the Latin word "*Moneta*", a name for Juno, the Roman goddess of heaven. This posits why the Romans played an integral role in the creation and development of money. Records, however, have it that the actual conceivers of money could be traced to Lydia, a city in Asia Minor or today's Turkey. The activities of their government at that time saw to the invention of minted money and this boosted the economy of Lydia. From the activities recorded at Lydia, other countries began to lay credence to the use of money coins. They made similar coins and they thrived in its usage until the Roman government caused inflation at the peak of the first century AD.

The Roman government minted many coins to finance its military and this caused a huge devaluation of money. Users had to spend more as the value of one coin depreciated. This means that people had to carry more coins to meet their needs.

Gradually, there was invent of paper money which was used by private lenders and merchants for centuries until France, in the eighteenth century, formally standardized the use of government issued notes. This was quite a controversy at the time. Paper money meant that government no longer had to use gold or silver in the minting process. They could create value with a printing press; albeit, they had to physically back the paper up with reserves of gold.

Today, money has taken various stages of development and has existed in various forms. Its value has, at one point or the other, increased and at the other point, reduced. Man, however, tends to have an intertwined relationship with money and cannot be separated from the subject. Little wonder why Jane was drained in confusion; money confusion.

As a young woman, she never believed that she was going to be stuck in financial crisis. She thought she had the best of life until it dawned on her that she was spending a huge part of her income. Her problem was not that she did not earn good money. Her monthly income measured to the tune of eight hundred thousand naira but that was way lower than what she had spent ten days into the month.

Her father, who handed the company over to her, would never believe that she did run it into severe debts. She had heard of corporate firms who run into debts and get sold off to their competitors in order to save the heads of their investors. "This is exactly what is going to happen to Graneal Foods Ltd if care is not taken." She thought and sighed. She wished she could turn back the hands of the clock and save herself the whole embarrassment.

It was there on the breaking news the night before that a once-flourishing bank was going to be sold out or rather, be bought by another bank. This is exactly how the news of her company's doom will be announced if her greatest fear came to pass. She could remember how her father had to hand over the leadership of the company to her on her 30th birthday after having her promise that she was going to ensure the smooth running. Her graduation as an economist gave her an edge when her father decided to stay away from business and have another person run the activities of the company. But did her academic qualification really keep her off her worst fear?

She decided to take action immediately. Her mistakes, actions, and corrective measures taken are what you will get to find out as you read through the pages of this book.

MONEY MOVES. USE IT RIGHT

Man faces a huge problem when it comes to things of money. More reason he has to be updated on the models and formulae to stay financially-crisis free. Nothing keeps a man at pressure than the thought of piling up huge debts. That alone can cause one to take drastic decisions with adverse effects on his health and emotional life.

Understanding financial freedom to be automatic is possible if you take the rules and principles of money to heart. This is what every individual, especially entrepreneurs, should understand. Nothing should limit you from making money and building wealth. However, have you taken time to ask yourself, "Why can't money stay in my hand? Why has there been movement of money from hand to hand?"

Money movement is seen in how individuals receive and spend money. Money comes and goes. Have you held money in your hand and the next minute, you'll begin to wonder what you used it for? Sometimes, you might go to shop for stuffs after which you get confused over what you really used your money for.

A female friend once shared her story some time ago. She had prepared for work, ensured that her kids were off to school, saw her husband off to his car, hopped into her car and made for her office. As soon as she reached the office, she dropped her bag beside her table and began to work. She had an urgent call from her boss for a meeting scheduled in an hour time. When she came back, she discovered that her bag was open and some money missing.

According to her, 'This has been happening for some time' but at that point, she couldn't bear it anymore. She had to spill it. Everyone was surprised because such a thing has never happened in their office. Luckily enough, the entire company premises was under CCTV surveillance. The security department made for the captures that morning and discovered that no one touched her bag and besides, she left it open before going to meet with the boss.

She had to check herself to ascertain how she had spent her money. On close observation, she discovered that she was the one who took the money, spent it, but did not remember that she did. I couldn't laugh enough at this story but this is exactly what happens to you when you are not careful with the money that comes into your hand.

Your manner and attitude towards the movement of money agrees to the fact that money comes more to people who use it right. If you tend to use money right, you will always have it come your way. If you use it wrongly, it will keep going away from you.

Money movement did not start today. When there was no physical money years back, people still had to buy the things they needed. The medium of exchange then can be described as the Trade by Barter System. This was the system used before money was introduced. The system allowed for exchange of goods nearly equivalent in value. People exchanged their goods for their needs. However, one of the challenges of this trade system was the inability to find who needs what you have and have what you need.

Gradually, paper money came into existence just like I mentioned earlier and that eased the problem of want and need disparity. However, most people see the paper money as the real measure of their wealth. This has caused them to place more value on the physical money but ignore the knowledge to invest and build wealth. Unfortunately, the problem lies in the mindset with which man approaches the issue of money. In the next chapter, we will see how the mindset affects the ability to make and keep money.

CHAPTER 2

THE MONEY MINDSET

Jane could not believe that she was broke. "Could it be that I spend too much lately?" She questioned as the telephone rang. It was her secretary calling to remind her of the meeting the company had scheduled with the bank in three hours time. It had been two days since her account manager sent her a mail. Now, the company's bank management wants to have a meeting with the company's financial team.

Two weeks earlier, she had been shopping her way not minding the threat-signal that loomed around. The financial growth of the company was clearly on the lower slope and if nothing was done, something she dreaded would happen. Sadly enough, this was not her thought when she bought two cars in less than one year. She had seen the car model from the auto company's new release brochure online and placed an order not minding that she just bought a car three months back. Not just that, she never misses shopping sprees with her friends. This made her question her qualification. "How did I go this far even as an economist?" For her, money has become a mystery she cannot explain.

When attempting to master the principles guiding money, you must understand that the success of such action lies in how much your mind perceives the subject to be. Does the mind see money as something worth having or does it see it as an illusion or would I say, a mystery?

Money has become a confusing subject of discussion over the years. This is more reason money is being seen to be an illusion. The way it gets into one's hand this minute and slips away the next minute remains a mystery. The unequal distribution of money makes it difficult to understand who it was really invented for since it tends to favour a particular set of people.

The ability to make money is further established by the attitude of those concerned. Making wealth is one thing and keeping it is another. This is where the mind plays a big role. The way you perceive money determines if that money will birth more money or if it would go down the drain. Your money mindset tells how successful you will become in staying out of debt and achieving your financial goal.

This mindset covers your entire perception about money. It affects how you take financial decisions. What you think about any issue becomes the bedrock for recording success in that issue. If you have a poor mindset towards money, be certain that you will run into financial problems as the day goes by. If you have a positive thinking towards money, you will get to make better choices to avert financial challenges.

IS MONEY REALLY AN ILLUSION?

One point to consider when discussing the issue of money is to know why people see money as an illusion. Money is merely a legal tender; a form of exchange used to weigh value. It represents the value of anything. It is the 'body' of value; a physical representation of value. It gives insight to what an object or service is worth and helps owners of those products and services exchange them without feeling ripped off.

Whenever the subject of money is raised, the seeming view of it being an illusion is based on the fact that it is different from wealth. Some see wealth as that cash in their hand, bank account, or the cost of the things they buy. This is where the illusion arises from. Unfortunately, most people do not understand that for one to have a proper knowledge of wealth, he or she must know what money truly represents.

Mere looking at the cash in its physical form is like looking at a shadow. Wealth is not the cash you have in your hand neither is it the notes in your bank account. Physical money is not wealth. Besides, that physical money is not healthy for your financial state either. It creates a picture, very obscure, that you fail to act on the principles and rules of money. "After all, isn't this money in my bank account?" You may think.

At that point, you will begin to see yourself as someone who is rich; of course you are. Rich people make claims to physical money. Wealthy people make claims to assets that can bring them money in the long-run.

VALUE BRINGS MONEY

It is possible to see a young man who wants to make money but have nothing to offer in exchange. His mindset already tells him that he needs money and must make it. When it becomes clear that he wouldn't reach that half-baked goal, he resorts to get-rich-quick schemes and gimmicks.

As an individual who seeks financial freedom, your mind and attention should be fixed on the value within you and those around you. There should be a symbiotic flow of value between you and the people you meet on a daily basis. That value is what brings the money. Value attracts money. A step to increase the value you have is a step to increase your worth. When you develop the value in you and in those around you, the physical money corresponds to that action.

This is not to say that those who are poor do not have value. They sure do but the difference between a rich and poor individual is that the rich guy decided to exercise his brain and work on the value he has. He knew that his internal value wouldn't breed result if it was not acted upon. Intrinsic value doesn't bring the money. The value acted upon does. The rich guy has a higher internal value than the poor guy and until the poor guy decides to work on his value, he will keep seeing money as an illusion.

THE POOR MONEY MINDSET

Your mindset is what drives you to take action on any issue confronting you. Your money mindset isn't away from this. The mind creates what I refer to as *wealth consciousness*. This shows how enlightened you are in issues relating to money. It shows if you are ready for a financial lift or if you are comfortable being stuck in that money position you find yourself in. The mind acts on the consciousness it is exposed to; more reason it is said that most people's inability to earn more started from their mind.

A poor money mindset keeps you in fear of taking decisions. It makes you feel intimidated each time you stand out to prove your point. If you were to invest in a particular project, as an individual with a poor money mindset, you may end up giving flimsy excuses of fear of risks which of course you know money entails. If you must make money, you must be ready to take risks.

On the other hand, one might feel that if he or she does not measure up to a particular spending capability, he would be looked down on. Unfortunately, the fear of getting intimidated by peers or colleagues have left many in debts. Check those who are affected by the fear of intimidation, you will discover that they freak at every new invention and try to measure up irrespective of their earnings.

Competition is another emotional backdrop that makes humans feel the need to be abreast in all things. In this case, people tend to stage financial competitions among themselves. Most times, these competitions are clearly staged and other times, the mind stages the competition itself. Too bad if your mind stages a competition with another who does know that you are trying to measure up. It is as good as saying that you are competing with your mind.

Another distinct feature evident in individuals with a poor money mindset is the inability to take quick financial decisions. They get stuck in decision making that they lose money. Unfortunately, they make bad choices when it comes to money because their mind perceives it wrongly. What differentiates the poor man from the rich man is the understanding of money. Unlike what is generally held, you cannot earn more if your wealth consciousness hasn't been conditioned to see money as a physical object and not value.

THE RIGHT MONEY MINDSET

My definition of the right money mindset is embedded in wealth consciousness. Understanding the capability to make money irrespective of situation is what shows that you have the right money mindset. One edge the right money mindset gives an individual is being able to covert wealth consciousness to physical cash. This is where the internal value man has plays a role.

When you have the right money mindset, you wouldn't be perturbed about what the seeming exchange rates read because the value in you will sure equate your cost. All you have to do is work on your value and the money will come. The people you see as rich or wealthy did not rise to that level in vacuum. Something preceded their rise. They had goals which only those with the right money mindset could work towards. Not only did they have goals, they were able to spot opportunities and grab them irrespective of the risk it posed. Those with the right money mindset do not only depend on their goals, but seek ways to accelerate their money journey.

The right money mindset makes you think possibilities always. Even at stages where it seems as though you will fail, it keeps you going. You will be so immersed in wealth consciousness that money begins to follow you automatically. Not just the physical money but the intangible value that comes with wealth. When this happens, you will experience that freedom. This is what the right money mindset can give you.

In the next chapter, we will understand what money really is and how it works.

CHAPTER 3
UNDERSTANDING MONEY

Jane needed to clear her head of the looming threats that came from the company's investors. Most of them could sense the danger – bankruptcy. The Finance Department of Graneal Foods Ltd was experiencing what she described as 'the toughest period ever'. She could not understand how the multiple zero figures that were recorded from their many successes in the past weren't visible in the company's account anymore.

She picked up her phone to call Michelle but thought against it. She was the wrong person to call at that moment. All the girls knew her; immediately after the pleasantries, the next thing would be "When are we going for a champagne party with the other girls or when are we going for shopping?" Jane had once shunned her for not wanting to hear what the person who called her has to say before asking for party and shopping details. It was not her fault; she was married to a man who insisted that she became a house wife as he could provide all she would ever need. That alone has caused her understanding of money roll to become 'an object to get the best of life'.

Talking about money can be quite confusing when such discussion happens to be with a person who relegates it to the background. Such person can make you look stupid and in most times, confused too. Knowing that money has great connection with a good number of factors that affect man, it should be treated not as 'the all' but as a factor that can shape the standard rate of living.

Money is the biggest of all drugs. It is a drug and the lack of it or its overdose can cause an individual serious financial damage. This is more reason you need to understand money and be financially knowledgeable about how it works. Factors like network, moral beliefs, and spirituality go a long way to shape man's understanding of money. The way you treat these factors will sure reflect in your financial life. We can agree that our attitude towards our network, lifestyles, and beliefs affects our stance towards money. This implies that man's reluctance to pay attention to these factors will affect his money circle.

In the aspect of network, proper attention paid to relationships makes them grow. The network built is what sustains the parties involved. It is said that you are the average of the five people you hang out with most. So, if you hang out with millionaires, you are on your way to becoming one and vice versa. Stay with people who think that it is difficult to make money and you will find it difficult to make money.

Your network should be properly checked if you want to grow your finance and build financial freedom. Hang out with people who come up with smart business ideas. The more time you spend with them, the more active your brain becomes to thinking the way they do. You cannot ignore the efficiency of network when it comes to the issue of money. Your network determines your net worth.

Another factor is moral beliefs. The way individuals view life is different hence their take on most moral issues. If one happens to see extravagance as a way of life, such person might experience crisis in his financial life. Same happens in religion. One's religious belief, to an extent, affects his or her understanding of money. If you think that shouting "ah ah" to every words of a preacher will grant you eternity, then your perception of money will be that of praising the wealthy hoping to get money.

It is very easy to see people ask a thousand and one questions on how to get money but go back to bed each time they see needful information to work with; such a cynical act! To these people, it will be better if the process is limited to just a click on a button and money will begin to pour out. Their understanding of money is conditioned in the sense of 'make the money and spend it'. No wonder the get-rich-quick schemes are flaunting their subscription details everywhere including on the Internet. The unfortunate ones click immediately and get started on the journey to making 'big money quick'. Doom!

Truth be told that it is easy to make money in this case but such money which was made without value would not be of value either. A quick glance at those who get rich through these schemes shows that their perception towards money is that of callousness and extravagance. Such money does not last.

IS MONEY THE KEY TO HAPPINESS

Those who do not understand the principles and standards behind making money might think that the little they know about being rich is all they need to make money and when they eventually earn a little token, they brandish it to suit the perception they once had. When a little sum of money happens to get into the hands of such people, they spend it as though that was all they ever needed to live. This set of people begins to see money as the key to happiness. They ignore the aspect of striking a balance in life.

A young man who rushes to buy a car worth over 10 million naira will someday wish that he invested it in assets not liabilities. Sadly enough, that was his definition of happiness; riding a big car. Few years from now, that car will be outdated and his happiness, diminished. Same applies to a young woman who spends more of her funds on her closet and hair rather than on assets. She will, someday, see those things she spent her money on as outdated.

Do I talk about those who feel that they are not a part of this life as they are not wealthy? They can take whatever quick means to make money and in that manner, spend it. The understanding of money, to these people, needs to be emphasized on. Not only are they confused, they have a long way to go for their distorted mentality to be corrected.

We need to understand that most people are poor not because they are not making enough money but because they lack understanding of the principles and rules of money. It is true that money is needed to grow relationships and live good lives but it should not be seen as the bedrock of happiness. You can be happy without bringing money into the picture. Yes, you can.

NEVER AN EXCUSE

Bimbola took a decision to save for a project she wished to embark on in a few months' time. She had, prior to when the idea struck her mind, felt that saving money was not necessary. That notwithstanding the fact that she earned more, she also spent more than was required. She was in the same situation as Jane. Having no money was not an excuse," She assured herself.

When she got the project idea and was about to kick off, she couldn't because her financial capability was not welcoming. She had to push the project further and that caused her a huge loss. She told her friend, Jane about it and confessed that she never knew that such idea would come by talk more of the international opportunities that were attached to it.

As situations like this come to scene, we tend to see how the excuse of ignorance holds us from taking charge of an opportunity. A lot of people have missed out on opportunities because they do not have the financial commitment required of them. Check thousands of youths today and they will tell you that they do not have 'travel money'. Not because they are not earning but because they are not saving. A person who got an opportunity to pitch to international organizations might miss out on his luck because he cannot fund his trip. A person who needed to attend conferences and seminars would be held back by lack of finance. There is always opportunity for those who are prepared. It is better to be prepared before an opportunity comes than wait for an opportunity before getting prepared. One way is to have money to access these opportunities.

Ignorance is no more an excuse in the 21st century. Lack of financial knowledge is the reason most people miss out on opportunities. They work hard but aimlessly. When faced with financial crisis, they claim not to know that such was capable of happening. Do not fall into this well of ignorant people. Learn and be open to learning more. Prepare for opportunities so that when they come, you can grab them with both hands.

KNOWLEDGE PERMITS CONTROL

Basically, it is a verified fact that one cannot be in control of what he or she lacks adequate knowledge about. For instance, if you purchase a generating set quite obscure in its model and difficult to operate, wouldn't you find it confusing in terms of technical build up? This means that for you to operate the set seamlessly, you need a manual or instruction document or better still, have an expert show you how to do it.

Financial control is one aspect every individual must strive to attain. You should be able to make decisions and enforce them. The only way this can be done is by understanding the workability and possessive nature of money. You cannot claim to be in control of your finance if you lack knowledge of how things work. There should be a consistent gulp of knowledge by any individual who wants to know better and attain financial freedom. Continuous exposure to knowledge keeps you at the top of the game wherever you find yourself. The more you know, the more you are in control.

THE SMART MONEY IDEOLOGY

The first step to understand money is to know that money is nothing. It is just an agreement form of measurement for value. Economics teaches that money is anything approved by the ruling authority to be a medium of exchange for goods and services. This means that asides the approval by the government, money is nothing. Further implying, anything can serve the purpose of money inasmuch as it is legally approved.

Whenever a particular object takes up the job of measuring value and aiding transaction, it becomes money. When it stops performing that duty, it returns to the ordinary object it is. Hence, the idea of having the physical money and stocking it is heart-breaking. What if those commodities you are hoarding become ordinary tomorrow?

Money holds no value when it is not invested. Hoarding money is also a way of saying 'I don't think you are worth investing' and that hampers growth of both the individual and the money. Giving much attention to the physical money is another way to drive yourself into financial crisis. Think real money. Think about how you can get that paper money to bring you consistent income.

The smart 21st-century entrepreneur knows that there are smart ways of making more money. The advent of technology and the Internet is one quick way of boosting one's visibility and multiplying his or her income. Very few understand this aspect of money making and that few are the smart ones who are gradually taking over the digital space monetizing and profiting from what they know and can do. As long as I am concerned, the Internet has made it easy to earn more.

DON'T BE RICH. BE WEALTHY

Money will be well understood if we differentiate it from riches. What most people refer to as being rich is having large physical money to throw around. Having a steady source of income doesn't mean that you spend at will to prove that you are rich. Money management is what posits you to be rich. When you make #350,000 monthly, how do you manage the money? For some people, it is easy to earn more money but difficult to manage that money.

Lack of money management skill can cause one to go into financial crisis. It is clear that such person lacks knowledge of how to direct money to ensure steady cash flow. Mastering how to invest properly is one way to become wealthy. The level of wealth one has is measured by his asset accumulation and not money accumulation.

This agrees to the idea that one might be wealthy but hardly spends cash. The fact is that they invest their cash into assets to boost their wealth. However, those who see money as being rich spend unapologetically and go into debts. This was the case of Jane who ruined all her father had built because she lacked knowledge of the difference between wealth, riches, and money.

One way to measure wealth and build financial freedom is to know your net worth. That is the difference between the estimated value of your assets and liabilities. If your asset is more than your liability, your net worth will be positive and that defines you as wealthy. If negative, you are just rich.

I know a young man who bought a car to add to his fleet of cars. This same man has no land or any landed property. What do you think will happen to him when he begins to experience financial backslide? What would happen when the physical money he has is nowhere to be found?

It will get to a point when increasing your net worth gives you an edge and one way to achieve this is by reducing your liabilities and increasing your assets. You should think sustainability if you want to avoid financial crisis. Anything that will depreciate in few years to come should not be your priority. You should not buy a car of #10,000,000 if your annual earning is #15,000,000. That is more like throwing your money to the swine. Instead, look out for an asset class that will multiply your income when invested into.

Wealthy people understand this. They understand the difference between how they earn and how they spend and ensure to strike the balance. They know that being wealthy implies how many days one can survive without an additional income without necessarily living below his standard. You cannot claim to be wealthy and go low on your standard of living when all means to earn more are blocked. If you spend more than 50% of what you earn, you are some miles away from bankruptcy.

This means that for you to be wealthy, you must increase your income and curtail your spending habit. If possible, check if what you will be spending your money on is an asset or liability. This is what differentiates you from that person who anticipates the next month's salary in a month that has barely gone half. Rich people and wealthy people are easily recognized from their spending habits. Don't be rich. Be wealthy.

KNOWLEDGE EQUALS UNDERSTANDING

As an entrepreneur, my knowledge of money has grown based on the experiences I have encountered. I have come to understand that you don't necessary have to show that you are rich by spending on liabilities. You can spend to become wealthy. Knowledge will teach you this.

It is now easy to make money as smart marketing strategies keep springing up as the day passes. Unfortunately, the aim isn't just to make money but being able to spend it right. You must know how to build sustainable wealth by investing in assets. Unfortunately, most people who want to leverage the smart ways of making money lack this knowledge. This is why they run into debts as soon as there is a shift in their cash flow. They get frustrated when their online space experiences a little glitch.

While assets bring you money as each second passes, liability drains you of your money. By now, you should know that your physical money only makes you rich. You get wealthy when you invest it in profitable ventures. These are the real money-making machines. Robert Kiyosaki once said, "Assets feed you while liabilities eat you". You see why it is necessary to have proper knowledge of money.

Proper understanding of what money is depends on the knowledge its owner has about it. You cannot aspire to be wealthy but lack the right knowledge to achieve it. It is like someone who wants to go global without knowing that he needs a passport. Seek the right knowledge.

SOLVE A PROBLEM. EARN MORE MONEY

The easiest way to make money is to provide a solution to the many problems man face. This involves sharing what you have with others and having them appreciate you for doing so. This brings you to the spot of selflessness as your main aim isn't just to profit but to be a source of relief to others. You make the process easier and sweeter.

Man's purpose in life is to affect his immediate society positively. That is where your internal value becomes activated. You will find out that you do not only become productive but you will also begin to see a new line of action to be taken in the pursuit of life's purpose. You will, in due time, begin to get amazing accolades in the tune of cash not just for being selfless but for being a person of value. It does not stop there, you will feel fulfilled being the reason a smile was planted on someone's lips.

Earning comes from solving a problem. If you get into an environment and you discover that something is amiss there, the earlier you find a solution to it, the better your chances of turning it into a profitable means. Solving your neighbour's problem does not only bring you money. It posits you as a figure to be emulated and respected. People will begin to look up to you. This should tell you that you can make money and still impact the world.

MONEY AND RISKS

The need for money security is what keeps a lot of people from trying out smart ways of making money. This is to suffice that people do not want to take risks and thus, would prefer to keep that physical money handy and in sight. What this births is a group of people who see themselves safe because they have their money with them. Unknown to them, they are moving towards financial crisis.

Life, on its own, is a risky adventure. Anything you do in life is risky. You wake up one morning and decide to set out on a journey; do you know that anything can happen? That is exactly how money systems work. You have to take risks, fail, and try again until you get it right than staying away from risks. You cannot afford to wait until you have the whole money before you can invest. Taking risk to invest the little you have is one step to becoming wealthy. I wrote this book to you believing that it will serve its purpose. That is risk-taking. I would have decided not to write a book and keep my knowledge to myself because no one might buy the book. But it is right in your hands because I ignored the fears and took action.

You need to understand that money is risk and earning more money implies taking more risks. When you decide not to take risks, your income flow begins to diminish and the result always turns out to be something you wouldn't like to see. The person who risks nothing does nothing, has nothing, and becomes nothing. His growth is stunted when it comes to his financial state. He remains who he is each passing day.

Remember, the difference between a successful person and a

failure isn't the ideas the former has but the courage he has to take calculated risks and act on it.

NO ONE OWES YOU MONEY

The reason a good number of persons do not have money is because they expect a lot from others. They expect their parents, family members, and friends to give them money. They are hooked in the Entitlement Syndrome. This is one reason a young man wakes at morning, takes breakfast, goes to visit friends, talk about irrelevancies, come back home, eat, sleep, play around, and then expect manna to fall from the sky.

In times past, people had opportunities to wield wealth because they knew someone who was born into royalty or related to a wealth person. Others were born with a silver spoon and were accessible to wealth and connections that bring wealth. Today, things are slightly changing. It isn't how it has always been.

Today, wealth opportunities are open to as many people who are ready to grab it. The 21st-century money is now accessed by as many who have got knowledge of what it takes to get it. There is no more restriction to group, social class, or gender. The accessibility of money was enabled by the invent of technology and the opportunities brought to man by the Internet. The criterion, in this case, becomes being able to spot these opportunities and maximise them. Commanding great influence and giving value using these machineries is an indication that you can position yourself for wealth.

The entitlement syndrome is now left for lazy and unintentional individuals who want their family and government to do everything for them. They would rather beg than learn a skill. They would rather opt for Ponzi schemes than look for ways to make money and sign up with reliable investment schemes. A lady once got stuck in one of these get-rich-quick schemes. She was supposed to pay her rent but thought otherwise and 'invested' her rent fee. "I will get ten times the money from this investment. I will pay the rent and invest the remaining money". Her thoughts were filled with what she would do with the money when she gets it.

It wasn't easy to console her when she heard that the site for the so -called investment had crashed. "How would I pay my rent now?" She lamented. She decided to ask her friend for money. This same friend had advised her to ignore those schemes but she adamantly 'invested' her rent fee. Now, she feels bad that her friend do not have money to give her.

Entitlement syndrome has made a lot of people lose opportunities to make money the right way. They feel that they need money at all cost; money was supposed to be theirs after all, but they ignore the rules to making money. They feel that Ponzi schemes are easier and faster ways, hence their decision to opt in. Maybe you need to ask yourself, "Who are the founders of those schemes? How do they make the money they will use to multiply yours? What legal backings do they have?" Ask yourself these questions and see if you can come up with an answer pleasing to the ears. Why then do you think those scammers owe you anything? They are only playing on your gullibility.

The more you place your hope on your family, friends, government, or even money-doubling agencies, the more confused and frustrated you will become. No one owes you anything; not in this century. The channel to make money the right way is widely accessible. Your decision to leverage it will determine your financial state years from now.

In the next chapter, you will be shown how money works in line with the psyche.

CHAPTER 4

PSYCHOLOGY OF MONEY

Jane was loath to admit that her money fear was overwhelming her. She could not come to terms with the fact that her friends and family members think that all is fine. Sadly enough, she could not talk to anyone about it. It was only the staff at Graneal Foods Ltd that knew that their money well was running dry. She had been wondering what the outcome of the proposal they sent to Hollisi Limited in view of the contract to supply fruit juice for the National Children Day celebration as their firm was contracted to manage the event.

As soon as she made for the telephone to talk to her secretary and ask her to provide details of the proposed contract they sought with

Hollisi Limited, her phone beeped. It was an SMS from Michelle. *"Hey girl! My sister-in-law had just sent her colour of aso-ebi for her big day. I hope you remember that her wedding will be coming up next month ending? She says that aso-ebi material costs #120,000. I will send you details of payment soon. Talk later."*

She read the message and sighed. "Not now! Not when I am at a compromising edge with the company's finance." She cried. This was the life she has been accustomed to; rocking every ceremony she gets an invite to in the best of *aso-ebi* with a classy shoe and bag to match. At that moment, she could not remember if that was the seventh or eighth *aso-ebi* she would be buying in less than six months. She had just finished paying for the Céline tote she ordered two Saturdays ago. "I can't allow people know that I am experiencing some financial issues at the moment. I will see how to do this and get my material before weekend." She spun in her chair.

WHY SHOULD YOU GET THAT *ASO-EBI?*

Jane's issue at that moment was getting the *aso-ebi* at all cost. What is your issue at the moment? That car, that bag, that shoe, that dress? Anything that makes you seek ways for self-gratification at all cost is that *aso-ebi* that you should not get. When it comes to the things of money, only a few are rational about it. We understand that saving and budgeting would be in our interest but we get carried away by the things we want that we fail to plan right. Our money behaviour becomes that of recklessness and exuberance.

Psychology of money aims to help you see money as a complex ideology that requires your commitment to building and nurturing. Your decision about money affects your financial state and creates an indelible mark on the path to your future. If you are not careful about what you spend your money on now, you will have to fight to foot your bills in the nearest future which is, of course, never what you intend for yourself. But you must understand that your attitude towards money in the present will play out in the future. This is a cycle which cannot be broken.

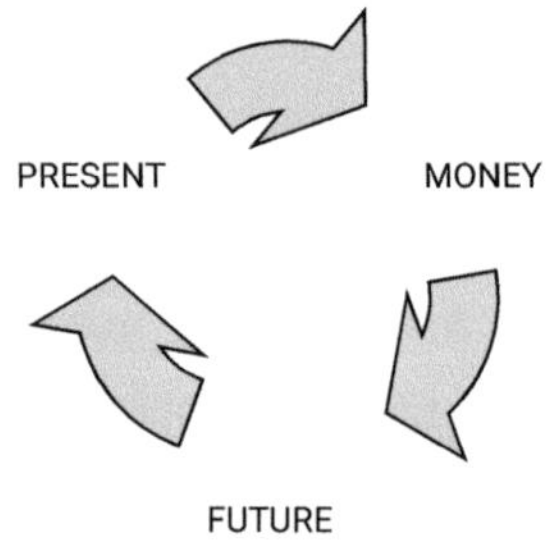

MONEY PSYCHOLOGY CYCLE™

Our problem most times is that we find a way to survive when there's no money but once money comes, we act as if our whole live depends on it. That is the **Money-Present Syndrome** most people face. They tend to lose self-control every time money gets into their hand. As shown in the diagram, the relationship between the three phases: money, present, and future is continuous. Want a better future? Start planning for it today.

MONEY AND EMOTION

Most problems we face in the course of making money and sustaining it is attributed to fear and guilt. These emotional attachments make us think irrationally. This, in most cases, makes most people feel that they are not meeting up. At certain point, one may begin to allow their emotions control them. This is exactly why that young man who earns #600,000 monthly still complains of lack of money.

Money management is possible when emotional management is achieved. Sometimes, the reason you go into debts is because you allow your emotions drive you. While most persons get attracted by shinny object, others allow themselves get trapped into buying unnecessary things even when they know that it would affect their income.

We must lend credence to the fact that the educational system did not teach us how to spend money. Although, they tried to tell us how to make money; which is an outdated model, knowing how to spend it was omitted. No wonder the educated ones are those who spend more. They lack good spending habits. They get carried away by what they see that they fail to apply rational thinking before taking action.

Have you ever wondered why you earn so much but still complain? Have you wondered why people work for years, retire, and still go begging? Have you tried to know why you can never have enough? The answers to these questions all have 'emotion' as their underlying factor.

There is this hidden force that pushes a man to do things especially ones that leave him in doubts. This force comes to full glare whenever it has to do with the issue of money. Each time you want to make a financial decision, you are tempted to think about the 'things' that you needed to spend your money on. Your emotions trigger you to see why investing that money may be a mistake you do not want to make.

Man's spending habit is triggered by his emotions. There is always a string of attachment to material things. There is this urge in man to show-off: buy new clothes, order classy meals, place orders for the latest gadgets, and book vacation spots at exclusive suites. All these are done to appease their yearn to live life to the fullest. As the normal Nigerian would say; "*This life na once*", man takes decisions on money with the same perception of 'enjoy now, tomorrow will think about itself'.

What am I trying to say? You cannot escape poverty if you are always spending above your income. You will go into financial crisis if your emotions drive you when taking financial decisions. The deal is not how much you make but how much you save. Saving comes with a lot of discipline. Maybe that's why it's only the disciplined that actually escape poverty. It is time to quit spending above your income. No matter how much you make, there should always be something to be saved.

YOUR LIFESTYLE VS YOUR SAVINGS

I know a young man who became a millionaire at the age of 26. He couldn't help but feel on top of the world. To him, all he had ever wanted was now given to him on a gold platter. He got a car worth millions of Naira, flew in business class almost every week, hosted parties, and rubbed the city with his affluent lifestyle. He would always remark, “I have experienced poverty and I cannot allow this time I have got to enjoy my money pass me by”.

Gradually, he spent his money on things that pleased his eyes until his bank account went red. I don’t need to tell you that he was back to square one few months later. Today, he is picking the pieces of his life but I am sure that the experience taught him a great lesson.

There is always this urge to spend money each time it gets into your hand. Maybe you have been in abject poverty some time ago, and seeing such freedom, you decided to savour the period while it lasts. You will not only run out of cash again, you will go back to the stage you were back then, but this time, with great sorrow and depression.

Our emotions have a way of pushing us. As humans, there is this attention we place on our emotions that has bad effect on our general well-being. A man who wants to satisfy his urge to ride on a costly car would do that as soon as he gets the exact amount of money in his account. Meanwhile, he fails to realize that it isn’t his emotions that will fuel the car and oversee its maintenance. What kicks in next? Financial crisis!

Do not get me wrong. It is right to seek the pleasures of life but that shouldn't be to the detriment of your financial life. You need to be knowledgeable about your net worth. Your liabilities should not be more than your assets. You should not spend your money on things that do not bring money. Your net worth will increase positively if your expenditures bring profits.

TEACH THAT CHILD TO EARN AND SAVE

When I was five years old, we would go to the bush to buy sugarcane with the little money my dad gave I and my siblings. We would cut it into bits, get a tray from my mother's kitchen, and start selling. We would sell at little cost and make profit. This is a childhood experience that keeps surfacing in my memory. As a young child, I started learning the nitty-gritty of money. My perception of money was conditioned and inculcated in me as little avenues to show my money skills came up and they were utilized. I saw money as a no-respecter of age or status. At that age, I understood that money multiplies no matter how small it is. I learnt the principles of money and worked with them to become a successful entrepreneur today.

It has been proven that children pick habits as they grow. Little wonder why children born into uncivilized environments take up habits they see exhibited by those around them. Same applies to money. If a child learns to save money from his or her early days, they grow to see money as something worth earning, saving, and growing into wealth. They won't spend the little they get instead, they will be so committed towards building streams of income. No doubt; you will see that child exhibiting good money habits in years to come.

Money invested is like a seed planted to be harvested in thousands of fold while the money squandered is like food eaten and its end product lies in the latrine. Same applies to good money habit. It is what your mind makes of money that comes into play when you have that money in your hands. Your perception of money affect the way you see it, spend it, invest it, and multiply it.

MONEY VERSUS PRESSURE

The typical 21st-century society puts a lot of pressure on individuals. This is ranging from overseeing the financial burden of the family and having to put up with your personal needs. The typical African society places a huge burden on those who they feel earns more than others. Unknown to these persons, they get welled up in the pressure that they begin to act accordingly. The man who fends for his immediate and extended family and also try to meet his personal financial needs will one day, get hooked in financial crisis if he does not check his money always.

I have seen young men take up responsibility for everything that needs financial solutions when it is clear that they are still starting out in their businesses. Unfortunately, money fleets. The result of this is the drastic effect it will have on their capital. Pressure can make you ignore your net worth while trying to carry the burden that shows up on a daily basis. That is dangerous for your financial health.

The reason some other persons fall into pressure is because they want to live a life not suitable for them. You will find this group of people putting themselves under undue pressure while trying to fit into the picture the society pulls to their face. At a point, they feel frustrated and try to end life by all means. You need to understand that these standards are not for you. You cannot be struggling to fit into a standard at the detriment of your bank balance. You do not need to put up an appearance that gives you sleepless nights. By all means, protect your psyche. For you to make more money, you need to be in a healthy state of mind.

MONEY MENTAL PROGRAMMING

When money becomes the bone of contention in any discuss, what plays in the minds of participants becomes "How will the money come?" On many occasions, it is written on the faces of these people. Little wonder why most corporate organizations insist on selecting the highly intellectual among them for such discussion. Money plays out perfectly in the mind before it comes to the physical. The perception one has about money goes a long way to determine if money gets to him or not.

I could remember how I had always envisioned money from my days as a little child. I had this belief of making money irrespective of what may come up. That belief alone was all I needed. This is same with most children born into a money-conscious home. However, those who never had this opportunity grew into a home that viewed money from a wrong perspective. While many had their minds wrongly programmed as kids, others allowed their environment and present situation condition the way they view money.

A good number of persons were told that they cannot achieve a particular level in life. This is the highest form of negative programming anyone can get. They began to grow with this programming. When opportunities to earn money and build wealth come by, they go into hiding. They fear risk and cannot see themselves investing the little they have.

The mental programming every man passes through goes a long in presenting a picture of him in years to come. Becoming successful lies in the ability to think and act right. If the mind at this point has been programmed to see impossibility, it will be difficult to get to the point of success.

Have you seen a man who gets a loan to start a business and in few months, was not able to account for the money? Check out, that person has a great tendency of being limited by his mental disposition. His mindset should be checked and corrected. The mind is the bedrock for any financial success. When you have the wrong perception about money, it finds its way out of your grip. The mind and money has a magnetic string attaching them. The more stable the mind is, the more value you are set to give in exchange for money, and the more the possibility of getting more money comes your way. When the mind's view of money is poor, the force with which it pulls money becomes weak and that means losing money each time it comes your way.

If you have a healthy view about money, you will find yourself attracting better opportunities to make more money. You will be offered opportunities on a gold platter and avenues to connect with those who will increase your income worth will be open to you. This is no magic. Your mind was able to pull those opportunities your way. However, if the case is vice versa, those opportunities will be repelled by the intents of your mind. Your mind determines the result of anything you do. This is why you should guard it jealously.

Check what comes into your mind on a daily basis. What words does your mind assimilate? What books do you read? Who do you network with? Yes! Your network affects your psychology of money. If you are around those who believe that they cannot make money, you will, unconsciously, begin to think like them. Your brain will accept all that is planted in it and the result each time the issue of money is mentioned would be the thought of not being able to make money. Like it is popularly said, "If you are in a group of four millionaires, you will be the fifth".

You should strive to keep up with the right psychology of money. Your attitude towards what comes into your minds should be that of strict scrutiny. Watch what you take in and ensure that those you connect with are those whose money ideologies are vision-provoking. Wealth creation requires that you think and act right.

When your mind is not fully mature to pull money, it repels it. That is bad for anyone who wants to build wealth in the 21st century.

THE PROGRAMMING STRATEGIES

Knowing that many have had their minds wrongly programmed, the right thing to do at this point is to have their minds corrected. This can only be possible when the right programming is done. More to this is the fact that as each day passes, the mind produces results of what it accumulates. If your mind's view is negative, it affects other aspects of your life. To correct this, attention should be paid to a number of strategies discussed here.

DISASSOCIATION

Continuous attachment to negative sources breeds an overhaul of negative attitudes. For you to change that negatively-programmed mind, you need to disassociate yourself from all that has traits of negativity in them. Staying around people who think the way you do only worsens the situation. The vibe to keep thinking that way; not believing you can smash your money goals and having a poor money mindset, is activated each time you get to share any money idea with them.

Have you been in a situation where you discuss a money idea with someone and that person keeps showing you reasons you should not go on with that idea? Most times, they analyse money issues in such a way that you keep seeing risks. This leaves you with multiple reasons not to invest. At this point, you need to take a step away from such person. Attachment to toxic networks amount to toxic personality duplication.

If you are someone who had the wrong programming about money, when you are in close contact with people who think like you, your already programmed mind clicks immediately and gets activated to act just as it is programmed. This is the point where you think small and only about how you will spend the little money you have on irrelevancies. This is just like an ulcer wound. If a person suffering from ulcer starts receiving treatment, he/she is advised to stay away from certain food contents. Failure to adhere to the instruction will cause the wounds to react and the pain at this point is usually unbearable.

A negatively-programmed mind is like an ulcer wound. When it keeps coming in contact with negatively-minded people, it gets worse. For you to reprogram it, you need to be around people who have a healthy mindset towards money. Your network should be people who pick on your money ideas and help you see possibility in achieving it. More importantly is the fact that you need to build a healthy money psychology if you want to breed a generation of wealth.

Have you wondered why the ability to make wealth tends to get transferred from some parents to their children? This is because these children had their mind conditioned from their childhood days to see money from a specific view. Closeness to their parents makes them envision the possibility of building wealth as soon as they come of age. This is not so with those born into poverty. Their view about money is so bad that it doesn't stay long with them peradventure it comes their way. They see money as 'come let's enjoy' and that is because they have been closely associated with like-minds.

A poor man who happens to have money in his hand will want to enjoy everything he felt he has been lacking. This is a wrong thought. What happens is that they get carried away that they forget that they needed to invest that money to build wealth. I call this **The Money Escape Syndrome**™. If they want to get reprogrammed, they need to stay miles away from those who think and act like them. The easy way to do this is by searching for those who think right and connecting with them.

POSITIVE DECLARATION

When your mind begins to get conditioned positively, the next thing that can help you activate your reprogramming is your declarations. I am one person who believes in speaking positively. It does not just help you get nearer to your financial goals; it helps you become confident of achieving them.

The words we hear and speak affect our mental state. It is not just about what we say to ourselves. I could remember a story of a young woman who felt that she was not doing the right thing by saving her money. She was always hearing her colleagues talk about the latest clothes and shoes they would order and each time, it seems as though she was not making the right decision. This is a lady who was trying to work on her financial life but the utterances from those around her were trying to infiltrate the reprogramming.

For one to begin to think right about money, their verbal propositions must align to this purpose. All that is heard and spoken must agree with this cause. It is the words of those around us that cause a trail on our financial state. For one to take a leap from the negative programming he/she once had, he must learn to speak positively about money.

I could remember a man who shared the story of how he spoke power affirmations every morning before setting out for the day. He said that he believed that if he could make as little as one thousand naira, he could also make one million naira. That was the magic with which he grew to become a wealthy man today. Can you say that to yourself?

In correcting negative paradigms infused into our mind by our background, we need to, first, understand that it is negative and not healthy. The earlier you notice such negative money psychology traits, the better and quicker you get at correcting it. At this point, all your utterances will begin to take a new facelift. You will begin to see yourself having that money, making huge investments, sourcing new streams of income, and empowering others to do same.

The mind is the center of consciousness and whatever it thinks about money shows out in words. Work on your utterances. Ensure they suit the new mindset you wish to imbibe. Think and talk about money always. Ensure your actions are in line with the words you speak. With time, you will get attracted to money as your words posited.

KILL THOSE MONEY FEARS

If you have ever been in want, you will not want to experience it again. There is this fear that arises when someone senses lack or has that feeling of not having enough to keep on with their lifestyle.

It often comes when financial crisis looms around. This particular individual may begin to see that they have been living above their income for a while and it is gradually eating into their financial state. At this point, they grip at the thoughts of the things they ought to sort out.

Fear on its own is a deterrent to financial freedom. When it grips you, it reminds you of that rent fee you haven't settled or the debt you are yet to deal with. It reminds you that your kids' school fees are yet to be paid and the family store needs a restock of food items. This can get you confused that you will begin to act reluctantly in setting more financial goals.

Confronting these fears is the best step to take. Take time to analyse those things that made you fall into this current situation. It might be that fashion taste you strive to maintain or that social lifestyle that has made you live above your income. The aim here is to identify these negative money habits and take up positive ones.

CONSISTENCY

Those who have the wrong programming about money tend to drop actions that can help them change. When this happens, such person goes back to who he/she was. There is need for consistency in reprogramming. Since this set of people has this inability to commit to money issues, they do not need to retreat if they really want to change. Yes, you need to be committed to this reprogramming process.

If you have ever tried to take up new positive habits like hitting the gym to get back to shape, you will agree with me that there is this urge to give up at certain points. It can be accrued to the inability to change completely but then, continuous exposure to the enabling environment would cause you to stay focused on the goal. This is exactly how money psychology works. The more you are focused in achieving a mindset-shift, the more you get better gradually. At a point, you will find yourself making financial decisions you never believed you would ever make.

Most times, the reason most people find it difficult to keep up to the cause for reprogramming is because the fear of their past keeps haunting them. If you have ever been told that you are a failure, you will begin to nurse same description when it has to do with money. That fear often materializes and when the time to make financial decisions come, you fret. You are alone in this journey and you must start thinking right. For you to get the right perception of money, you need to focus on what empowers you to think right.

APPROACH MONEY RIGHTLY

We pictured a scenario of a man who was born into poverty trying to enjoy life as soon as money came his way. It was just a 'breakthrough period' for him and this is the approach a good number of people born into the low class and middle class take when it comes to money. A poor man thinks that he earns little and so, do not have enough that can be invested. They see the little they earn as not being enough. This is in contrast to how a rich man thinks. The rich understand that their income can only bring more money when invested. They know how to draw a line between spending and saving.

If you must take a leap from falling into financial crisis, you must learn to approach money rightly. If you earn monthly, see the possibility of multiplying it. Most people just earn to save but the smarter ones invest. Savings is quite different from investment. If you are a 9-5 worker who earns a monthly income, your plan shouldn't be putting your money in a safe place like a bank where you get additional funds at the end of each financial month. However, when you invest, your money gets multiplied. I bet you know that there is a huge difference between addition and multiplication.

HAVE A PASSIVE INCOME

We have active income and passive income in the money world. Your active income is the money you earn from what you do. It could be a business or a job. Simply put, it is your monthly profit. If you are an employee, your active income is what you are paid. If you run a business, your monthly profit becomes your active income. Passive income is, however, the money you make from investments. If you are a stock broker, have landed property either on rent or lease, or have assets that bring money, the income from these ventures is your passive income.

Think multiple streams of income by allowing your money work for you while you sleep. Invest your money and create avenues for passive income. With such mindset, you will see yourself breaking boundaries and building a financial-crisis-free future.

Finding a lasting solution to your money psychological problem is possible if you can understand that money is a non-respecter of age. Your attitude towards money can only get better if you submit to learning financial rules. You need to understand that the first step to make money is to believe in the existence and multiplying effect of money. Interestingly, it is your ability to know more that will help you avoid cases that can cause you to fall into financial crisis. In the next chapter, we will see how certain myths limit us from making money.

CHAPTER 5
MONEY AND MYTHS

It was a sunny afternoon when Jane received a call from her dad. She was shocked. "Could it be that he had gotten wind of what was happening? Oh no, not now!" She thought. She got on the call and her dad's voice came without a trace of inquisition; no asking to delve into issues such as the one she was facing at the moment. He just wanted to inform her that her younger brother would arrive the country the next weekend and to inquire if she was coming to the house. "Of course! See you by weekend, Dad." As soon as she got off the call, she heaved a sigh of relief.

Jane checked her file for the details of the contract project the company had in view. She had hoped that the contract to supply fruit juice for the Children's Day Celebration event organised by the State government would be in their favour. She needed that money badly. The company did. The recent series of event flashing its ugly face down her thoughts have left her with many beliefs about money.

The confusion surrounding money has caused a good number of persons question certain issues concerning it. The tug fuelled at such situations cause them to grapple with the truths about money. The verified and unverified ideologies flying around us are capable of causing a crash of reasoning, and in cases where individuals pick on these ideologies, there is cause for alarm.

Most beliefs flying around are false and their infiltration into the minds of its hearers can cause a disruption in their proposed money chain. While most of these myths are centered on spiritual itineraries, others are borne out of selfish interests. The presence of these myths factors have become a challenge to those who want to build sustainable streams of income and get on board new monetization trends.

If you happen to be born and breed in a third-world country, you must have heard a lot of things that were capable of limiting your financial leap. There is a despondency that comes with the views and ideologies of individuals from these regions. These myths hold individuals from actualizing a set monetization plan. If proper evaluation can be done on these beliefs, man can live a financial-crisis-free life.

While some of the myths have a way of making man see impossibility each time he decides to change his money game, others try to show him why taking a step to financial freedom is not important. The biggest challenge the 21st-Century entrepreneur face is the tendency to agree with the myths of money. Most people do not know the truth about money. They have been made to believe the myths and ignore the truth they ought to pick on.

Money myths are beclouded lies told to hamper the proper usage of money and to hold individuals in financial chains. They are, however, taken hook, line, and sinker by the unfortunate ones who refuse to carry out proper money research. They get into the consciousness of these ones and alter their views about money. Only a few persons recognize this early enough to expunge it from their mind. These myths make individuals short-sighted whenever the issue of smart-money-making strategies are discovered.

Barriers to financial growth are evident in the society. The limitation to abundant wealth lurks around waiting for whom to hang on. Man's mind has been infiltrated with a lot of things. He has been told certain things about money and that has made him view money in an erroneous way.

At this juncture, you may need to search your mind for those beliefs you accepted. You need to seek ways to get it right now. The mind registers anything that comes into it. However, at this point, you need to reconsider these lies that have flooded your thoughts.

Many myths which fly around these days are often connected with religion. It is sad to know that most people have painted the truth about money to suit their malicious want and have infiltrated same in the minds of others. To achieve maximum financial freedom, the truth about money must be revealed. Some of the money myths include:

YOU CAN'T MAKE ENOUGH MONEY

When people try to take up smart ways to make more money, they are told that they cannot make enough. What this registers in the mind of such person is that no matter how much steps he takes, he would not make enough money. Normally, such person becomes lackadaisical towards **Wealth Accumulation™**. You can make as much money as you wish to. Be smart towards approaching money.

MONEY COMES TO THE RICH

There is this ideology most people hold these days. They see wealth as something that comes to the rich alone. They see themselves as the poor ones and believe that no matter how much they work, money won't get to them. So sad because the opportunities to make money are not far-fetched. The question here is, how committed are you to grabbing those opportunities?

DO NOT SPEND MONEY. BE A MISER

Most persons believe that for you to accumulate money, you must be a miser. You must avoid spending your money even on yourself. Unfortunately, many opportunities are unlocked with money. When you fail to spend to get them, you allow them slip into the hands of the smart ones. Also, most people would rather keep their money than use it to care for their health. With time, that money which was not used to care for their health will be spent in the hospital. This applies to all spheres of life.

DO NOT INVEST. IT IS RISKY

It has been largely said that investing into money trades and shares are sometimes risky. It is no news that smart people invest their money and watch it multiply. Others save and watch it add. Sadly enough, it is only those who take risks that get the key to unlock their track to wealth accumulation. Learn how to take risks.

I AM POOR AND IT IS HEREDITARY

People who have the hereditary limitation believe that they cannot be better than the background from which they came. "My parents are poor. My grandparents are poor. Poverty runs in my linage," They would always say each time they need money. To them, since their background was built on poverty, they cannot make money. Too bad!

MONEY IS THE ROOT OF ALL EVIL

The Christian Scripture admonishes that the love of money is the root of all evil. This has, however, been misinterpreted by various people as "Money is the root of all evil". They believe that for one to achieve eternal life, he must stay away from money. To them, the rich do not make Heaven.

Inasmuch as we were asked not to love money, it does not mean that accumulating your money to build wealth is wrong. The love of money can be viewed from various perspectives but when it applies to seeing money as a means to get value, does it imply evil? A quick survey shows that the enlightened ones who understand this Scripture verse make enough money to finance the Body of Christ and the ministry of the kingdom. Money is a means of achieving the end and you should begin to see it from that perspective.

SPENDING IS OFTEN MORE THAN INCOME

This particular myth has made people spend recklessly. They believe that one's spending must always outgrow his income. Sadly enough, they do not know that the smart ones save before they spend. A good money habit will help you save more and spend right.

THE RICH AREN'T HAPPY

It is believed that those who are rich are not happy. This is what the poor use to comfort themselves. When you are rich, you can get everything you want. Your happiness won't be compromised based on the fact that you cannot afford what you need. Poverty can, however, make you sulk at the miseries of life.

ACADEMIC QUALIFICATION DETERMINES ONE'S WEALTH

While the naive think that acquiring all the certificates in the world can make them rich, the smart ones know how to leverage those qualifications to make more money. There are poor educated people everywhere. Do not be deceived. Learn the new system to make money.

I NEED TO GET A HIGH-PAYING JOB

I know a young man who kept giving excuses as to why he couldn't save. For him, his salary was too low to start saving. When he eventually got a high-paying job, he was also giving same excuse. You don't have to be rich or paid so high before you save or invest. The truth is that poor money habit will always push you to financial crisis even with that high-paying job.

PAPER MONEY IS THE REAL MONEY

It is sad to know that most people think that paper money is the real money. Sadly enough, the real money is the investment you make that brings in money consistently. Paper money only makes you rich. Money when invested will bring you wealth.

HOARD THAT MONEY-MAKING KNOWLEDGE

Most people do not like to share the knowledge they have which can boost their influence and income. They will prefer to keep it to themselves. I heard a story of a young man who redesigned the logo of an auto company. He showed his skill and his work was endorsed. Others must have hidden their talent and message so that no one will know what they can do and copy them. However, the possibility of achieving result in any idea is dependent on the steps taken towards its success.

YOU DON'T NEED TO BE WEALTHY AS A WOMAN

Many women were sold this bullshit of an ideology. They were told that they ought to be in the kitchen and that no man would marry them if they are wealthy. Too bad because no man wants to marry a liability. Be an asset as a woman. Make that money.

YOU ARE STILL YOUNG TO MAKE WEALTH

This particular myth has become a source of relief for most young people. It is sad that people still place limitations on their ability to make wealth based on age. The founder of Facebook became a millionaire at the age of 22. Many young millionaires are emerging. You too can be one.

LIFE IS STAGE BY STAGE. GET A FAMILY BEFORE THINKING OF INVESTMENT

While the smart ones are investing to have a bliss-filled future, others are waiting to get married and have kids before they think about investment. Sadly enough, more people to look after, more expenditure. Invest now!

MAKE MONEY WHILE YOU SLEEP? NEVER!

A lot of people do not believe that they can make money while they sleep. For them, they must work hard and make money. The Smart Money Process is aimed at showing individuals how to make money while they sleep. With the advent of Internet, it is possible to have a system that credits your bank account while you sleep.

Learn that system.

HARDWORK IS THE KEY TO MAKE MONEY

Many people think that they have to work so hard to make money. They have to sweat and go down to the dust before they can make money. You may think that you have to hustle for money. These days, you can make money by working from home on your phone or system. Smart work is the way forward.

MONEY IS DIFFICULT TO MAKE.

The 21st-century youth think that they have to go into dubious acts to make money. They get beclouded by the stories they hear. Unfortunately for them, there are a thousand and one persons making money through decent means. Money is not difficult to make. It becomes difficult when you lack knowledge of how to get it.

EVERYONE MUSTN'T BE WEALTHY

I heard the story of a young man who felt that since his eldest brother was wealthy, he might not make money. He was consoling himself with the ideology that everyone mustn't be rich. This is exactly what most people think. To them, everyone mustn't have money. Too sad!

TALKING ABOUT MONEY IS A SIGN OF GREEDINESS

Many see talking about money as a sign of greediness. You are described as a lover of money and a greedy fellow if you make it clear that you need more money. Expenses are no respecter of poverty and the saga about greediness does not stop it from crashing at your doorstep. Talking about money does not make you greedy. Smart men discuss money ideas and map out strategies to make more money. Be one!

INSURANCE IS A WASTE OF MONEY

A lot of people will rather risk their assets than sign up to an insurance plan. They believe that insurance is a waste of money. The truth is that if you get on the right insurance plan and pay your premium as and when due, you are doing your assets great good by protecting them.

MONEY-MAKING IDEAS ARE PERSONAL

When people complain of lack of money, I try to know if they have knowledge of ideas that will bring them money. Sadly enough, they lack money ideas. One way to make money in the new system is by replicating another person's money idea and creatively creating streams of income. No money idea is new. Check out those doing well and do what they do.

I HAVE MONEY IN MY RETIREMENT PLAN

There is the urge to spend recklessly because you feel that you have enough money in your retirement plan. Have you tried to ask yourself, "What if something goes wrong?" Don't be overjoyed by what you have at hand that you fail to utilize it rightly. Be tactical about spending today.

DO NOT ALLOW THAT CHILD KNOW ABOUT MONEY

The typical African parents are overprotective when it comes to the issue of parenting. This is sad because most children who find it difficult to take financial decisions are actually those whose parents saw money knowledge as unnecessary. This makes a child who would have learnt the secrets of wealth from his wealthy parents grow to be daft and financially unintelligent. This is wrong. Teach young children how to manage money and build wealth.

There are a good number of these myths. The best thing to do at this juncture is to look within you and discern which of them describes your current financial state. These myths are inexhaustible and are greatly internalized. Those who have absorbed a good number of these myths tend to experience limitations in their financial life. Unfortunately, these myths are usually sold to us as kids and they affect our subconscious minds. Little wonder why most young people are afraid of taking financial decisions as adults. When you erase these myths off your mind, you will be able to identify the underlying factors that have hampered your financial growth all these while.

PHASE 2

HELP! I AM GOING BANKRUPT

CHAPTER 6

MONEY MISTAKES YOU MUST AVOID

Jane remembered one habit she took up few years ago. It was her reckless spending especially when the firm wins a project or records great sales. This was one habit that led her into spending so much that she failed to save. Whenever she remembers to save, it was often peanuts. There are a lot of mistakes we make. I have spoken about a few from the beginning of this book but I am dedicating this chapter to exposing all those mistakes.

When I started out in the business space, I had an idea that could amount to billions of Naira. It needed funding and as a young lad, I secured my ideas. Even when I was approached by investors to sell my idea, I refused. I was even offered #130,000,000 (Nigerian currency) to be a major owner of my idea but I rejected the offer. Today, I am regretting not accepting that particular offer. My biggest regret at the moment is refusing to sell the idea. I would have sold it and sure, more ideas would have been birthed and the proceeds would be used to boost the new ideas. With the knowledge of wealth creation I have amassed over the years, I would have done what Hellon Moz did with Paypal. He sold PayPal and today, he has a multi-billion dollar business which he has built out of the profit from selling Paypal. I would have sold my company's idea and built a multi-billion dollar business with the proceeds.

Just like me, a lot of people have made certain mistakes in their money journey. They start regretting when they see the effect of that mistake manifesting. This reminds me of Jane. She had started to trade Forex after studying the factors guiding the trade and mastering the processes involved in becoming successful in the business. She was vast in knowledge about Forex that her friends began to seek her advice when they finally decided to give it a trial. Her clear view of the underlying fundamentals made her envision a win in the business. One morning, she saw that a 'financial expert' was invited by a TV channel to speak on possible implementation of change in the country's exchange policy. She heard him say that it wouldn't be possible to have a change in the policy come so soon. To him, he was uncertain if foreign traders would get profit considering the state of the country's GDP.

Jane began to doubt her decision of trading Forex. The 'expert's' words confirmed her fears and that was how she panicky gave up on the trade. She abandoned her efforts in the last six months and incurred a loss to the tune of $450. Like a dream, the market was getting favourable, the exchange policy was becoming welcoming, and the prices were topping in profits by the day. That was a great loss for Jane. She would have been having an increase in her income if she hadn't dropped the trade because of what she heard.

Many money mistakes are lingering loopholes which were ignored in the past. As things began to change, it became disastrous to make such mistake in the 21st century. It is important that you avoid these mistakes if you want to make more money and stay off financial crisis. Some mistakes to avoid are discussed in the headings below.

LISTEN, THINK, ACT

In making money decisions, one thing you must avoid is taking action without thinking and weighing the possibility of getting it wrong. This is common among people who are afraid to lose money. They hear someone speak maybe at an event, interview, or on the media channels and instead of asking 'What is more to this?', they take everything hook, line, and sinker. Sadly enough, they lose more money acting on the unsolicited advice.

As a money-minded individual, you need to set your money guidelines when attempting to trade or invest in a particular trade. Your action should be based on the researches you have undertaken, confirmed, and have applied. It should be a compendium of your resolved opinion and it should guide you in making decisions relating to the trade or business.

Business evaluation should be made based on the facts you have and the number of successes and failures recorded in the trade. It shouldn't be an opinion you got or perceive to be right. Many businesses are going down the money drain because the owner ran the business based on the opinions he feel are conducive. Unknown to him, such opinions were not healthy for the business thus, leading to its death.

While making financial decisions, be sure to have a strategy to protect yourself and business from any loss. Learn to keep to the guidelines and extricate yourself from taking actions that will cause you loss. Stay put with your original strategy and do not be too quick to swap ideas because you heard someone say that it works for them. It would be better to win small than lose big.

WHEN CONFIDENCE BECOMES A CRIME

The trap that gets entrepreneurs into running loses these days is overconfidence. A quick survey shows that humans love to go by what they think they know or what they have experienced. This causes them to work with insufficient knowledge and run into great loss.

Stan is a wealthy business man. He has business structures in Real Estate, Forex, Oil and Gas, and other profitable sectors of the economy. He had made huge investment into his oil and gas business which had physical outlets in over five states. Few months later, he decided to go into another business. He saw that the business was blossoming but he failed to check well before investing in it.

Stan was confident that since he had done other businesses, there was no need carrying out a market survey to ascertain if it was wise investing in the business. This was how he went in, worked on speculations, and the business grew. Months later, there was news that the product would run into scarcity. This is the same thing that happens in the oil and gas sector and as usual, he decided to act 'smart' by buying the product in large quantity in preparation for the scarcity. He was sure that the price of the product would escalate soon and he would make enough profit.

Fast forward, the prices of the product started moving down because a competitor was up. This was against his initial speculation. The value of his investment began to shrink. Unknown to him, the speculation that the price would rise was the opposite of the situation in that particular market. He was too confident that he failed to understand the way the market was conditioned. He lost a huge amount of money because he was confident in the limited knowledge he had.

In an unstable economy, it is unwise to prove confidence in things relating to your money. You have to broaden your horizons if you must get it right always. Getting relaxed on what you know is one way to get it wrong always. You cannot afford to rely on knowledge which, sometimes, is outdated. When money comes into the scene, be humble to learn about what you are investing in. Smart moves are sometimes dangerous. Do not get caught in the web of an unstable economy.

THE SELF-WANT SYNDROME

A young lady wanted to get another source of income. She heard that selling female wears was the best way to go. She quickly reached out to two of her friends. The first friend told her that it wasn't the way she sees it. Selling wasn't that easy and for her to achieve success, she should try to learn the trade. The second friend told her to get started. According to her, the trade was going to blossom. She also told her that she can connect her to those who will help her. Cynthia got what she wanted to hear from the latter and ignored the former.

This is exactly what most people who want to invest their money face often. They want to hear what they want to hear and see what they want to see. Once they perceive a trade as the best, they see other people's views as unimportant. To them, the trade is blossoming when in the real sense, it is going low drastically. This should be avoided if you must keep your money safe. Do not be sugar-coated to agree to all you hear or see. Do not get entangled to your personal views. Look beyond the physical. Be smart.

UNREALISTIC EXPECTATIONS IN BUSINESS

One problem most people face when it comes to money is the high expectations they have. They anticipate unrealistic profits from a trade and this is caused by little wins in that trade. It is possible to see people who smash little goals in their business spend all the profit while waiting for a bigger win. Most times, they go ahead to borrow with the hope of getting money soon.

If you are into trading, avoid incurring huge debts because of unrealistic expectations. It is good to expect a win but do not go faster in spending when that win hasn't come. Profits from trade are not easily driven hence, do not hope to have a huge one that you fail to watch your expenditures. I have seen people who go into a particular trade and spend so much that their capital becomes affected. For them, they believe that the profit to come would save their ass.

Truth is that not everyone is fit to go into trade. Everyone wants to live the best of life but that cannot be achieved when your expectations are unrealistic. It is normal to be a boss but do not leave a job for trading because you feel that the profit to be gotten is high. There is also this urge to connect to the best of humans but do not ignore your family and friends in the course of doing so. They are the ones who will hold your hands in times of troubles. Do not seek a loan that is more than your fixed assets. By that, you put yourself at great risk. It is good to think profit but do not have high expectations that you fail to think right before taking decisions.

BECOMING AN EX

Fred is one young man who believes that he must enjoy life to the fullest. He failed to discern between what he wants and what he needs. He would host parties and spend lavishly trying to impress and attract unnecessary attention. He spent his money on liabilities and failed to invest in assets that could increase his passive income. He continued this way until he became an ex. An ex to money!

You will become an ex-rich person when you begin to act and think like Fred. The moment you begin to ignore financial security tips just to please your ego and show off, you will find yourself running to square one of your life. This is one mistake you must avoid if you want to live a financial-crisis-free life.

IGNORING FINANCIAL GOALS

Absence of goals makes you wake up to a future where you will discover that you have not achieved anything over the years. Many people today do not have goals talk more of financial goals. If you are in this case, how do you measure your successes and failures?

Lack of financial goals implies lack of insight. You do not only get hooked in debts, you might also not get out for a long time. If you want to live a stress-free life years from now, you must have SMART financial goals and actualize them. Your goals must be simple, measureable, actionable, realistic, and time-driven.

Let's say you have financial goals, how often do you review them? Are your goals that effective or do they need to be worked on? Do they suit your present state? Are your goals huge enough to accommodate your successes or do they limit you? Setting financial goals help you set parameters for your money and show you how best to spend it. Having to check every goal to ensure that they are worth achieving is key. You have to be realistic about every option before accepting them

Also, reviewing your goals helps you make better decisions in business and money-related issues. They help you determine what to trade on and why it is the most convenient to invest in. It helps you map strategies to actualize that big dream. Setting financial goals is the key to unlocking hidden opportunities in your business and financial life.

NO PLANS FOR RETIREMENT

A young woman who works in the bank for years shared her story as an undergraduate. She had worked in the Marketing Team and headed the unit at some point before her promotion to the position of the branch manager. While in the Marketing department, she was greatly blessed by her clients who would always leave cash notes as 'thank you' for her time and effort. Beautifully, she was well knowledgeable about money. She would put those notes into her money bank.

Her experience as a child taught her quite a good number of lessons. She didn't want to face such horrible experience again. Her father became a retired civil servant when she was in final year in the university. He never had savings. He would spend each month's salary and await the next. That was the routine in Temi's house and her father was unable to pay her school fees when he retired. He had placed hope on the pension he would receive as soon as the retirement came but the reverse was the case.

Temi couldn't explain how she came off the struggle of having to be in such financial crisis in her final year. Today, she shares her story whenever she was given the opportunity to do so. She advises her clients to have retirement savings plan. She knew that her father lacked financial intelligence that was why he allowed such befall him. Today, she sensitizes everyone who comes in contact with her to save smart and spend wisely.

The worst thing you can do as an individual is not saving for your retirement. I understand that there is this fun spending your 'hard-earned money' but it is wisdom to know that that money will not be readily available when you reach your retirement age. The strength and energy with which you work to make money will not be same forever. This is more reason you have to plan for retirement. While a lot of persons do not know that they need to save for retirement, others feel that their children will take care of them by then. What if the reverse was the case?

Actively planning and getting set for retirement is a smart thing to do now. Although, it seems far, begin to envision how you will meet your needs and stay out of want. Have a retirement fund account and ensure you top it every month.

This money mistake can cause you a lot of problems when you get old. Not only will you find it difficult to scale through old age, but you will get on financial crisis that will cut your happiness short. The smart thing to do now is to save while working so that you will not go broke when you stop working.

GETTING ONBOARD A TRADE YOU KNOW NOTHING ABOUT

I came across a publication in one of the dailies where the story of a young boy was shared. He had attempted suicide but for the timely intervention of his friend. The story had it that he got wind of a business which unknown to him was a Ponzi scheme. He saw the offers and opted in. He invested his entire savings with the hope of getting a huge return from the supposed trade. Few days later, he heard that the business site had crashed. He couldn't understand what they meant until he reached out to the person who introduced him to the business. As usual, the person exonerated himself from the loss and asked him to bear it alone since he also lost his money in the 'trade'.

Before you get onboard any business, ensure you do your research. Do not get carried away by the mouth-watering offers that you fail to carry out proper check. Do not put down your money for something that is at stake. This is applicable to people who start a trade thinking that it is the right thing to do. Most times, they end up in trouble. They cannot manage such trade. It is evident in how they get confused each time they are faced with challenges. Sadly enough, they entered such trade based on the opinions of people. They fail to plan and map out strategies to ensure effective business. They feel the trade was moving and hence, would be wise to get on board at that moment.

Understanding a trade will help you avoid mistakes. Seeing a trade moving well does not mean that you should go into it without proper planning. Sometimes, it is wise to stay a mile away and watch how things really work before getting onboard that trade.

GETTING ON A BAD DEBT

Debt might mean something bad to you but in real sense, there are good debts and bad debts. You need to understand these and be aware when you are about getting into a bad debt. A bad debt is one which requires that you pay from your earnings. It is bad because such debt was not able to finance its repayment plan. For instance, if you take a loan to buy a personal car, you are getting on a bad debt. That car is not bringing you money. You will get to pay back the loan from your earnings or retirement plan. This is so bad.

I have seen people take loans to go to school and acquire certificates with the hope of getting a good job. I have also seen individuals sell their properties to embark on a trip that will not bring any yield. The worst is seeing someone take a loan to finance a wedding ceremony. This is caused by lack of financial intelligence.

Meanwhile, you should know that if you work with an organization that pays you upfront, you are a debtor. If you place orders on credit, you are a debtor. If you access services and fail to pay utility bills as and when due, you are a debtor. The best thing to check at this point is if that debt brings you money or takes money from you. Is it to finance an asset or a liability?

You need to bear in mind that taking a loan from personal and corporate institutions is not advisable if you are not investing into something that will yield financial returns. The returns from such loans should be able to clear off the debt and not your earnings from your other income sources.

SPENDING WITHOUT PLANNING

Gbenga earns $800 monthly. He also runs a side business which brings him over $300. In total, he earns approximately $1100. He wanted to take a local flight to another town. The first class ticket costs $400 while the economy class ticket costs $100. In a bid to prove that he could pay for a first class ticket, he booked the ticket and that cost him a lot. He couldn't meet up to other expenses that showed up that month. A lot of people are spending more than what they earn. If you spend 50% of what you earn on something that wouldn't bring you money, it is same as throwing that money to the dogs. You cannot afford to spend your earnings on liabilities. I don't understand why people will make purchases worth over their monthly income. What then goes into savings? This is one mistake most people make. Spending less than what you earn is one important financial rule you must live by.

The easiest way to go into financial crisis is to spend without caution. Most people spend without planning. Little wonder why a man who earns in multiple six figures end up in lack before the next month's salary comes knocking. Most people live on their paycheque without taking time to articulate how much more such money could be put to use asides reckless spending.

Consciousness while spending is important for anyone who wants to stay out of financial crisis. You should be aware of what you spend your money on and if it is the best thing to do. You cannot watch your money go into wrong dealings. It is also unwise not to plan before spending your money. Any money that leaves your pocket should be directed towards something worth value.

SAVING AFTER SPENDING

Spending before saving has killed the financial dreams of a lot of people. It has rendered even those who earn large broke. There are people who do not spare a second whenever they get a credit alert. Their pocket leaks so much that they run into debts too quickly. Spending money is way too easier than saving. This has taken over the minds of most people that they fail to analyze their spending habit and improve on their saving habit.

When you fail to save, you plan to go broke. This is because you end up spending both on relevant and irrelevant things because you are still seeing the money with you. A smart way to stop this is by ensuring that you save a particular amount of money each time you receive your pay.

LACK OF A FINANCE BUDGET

Another mistake most people make is not having a finance budget. This implies that they spend without a clear view of what their financial statement is saying. Lack of financial budget will make you spend your business finance. Every business has its finance and should not be tampered with. Personal wants are met with personal finances. Business wants are met using business finances. If you use one for the other, you might likely run a loss in one aspect of your life. Too bad if it is in your business.

If you do not have a finance budget, your expenditures might likely run into your business finance which is not healthy for any business. Create a finance budget and stick to it. It will help you know when you are running expenses into your business finance and also help avoid your business running into bankruptcy.

PROCRASTINATION

This habit has caused a good number of persons to ignore important issues. I have seen a man who was to review a financial report procrastinate until it got to the late hour. Sadly enough, the review was done under pressure and the aim for it was not achieved.

Learn to put certain tasks away so as to have time to review your financial plan. Check out your goals for a month and map out strategies to achieve them. The more you procrastinate, the more you kill that dream. Taking action to see your financial goals being actualized will push you into doing more and setting bigger goals.

IMPULSIVE BUYING

Buying a particular product because it is the spur of the moment is one simple way to go broke and fall into financial crisis soon. In this case, you never had the intention of getting that product but because you see people getting it en masse, your emotions trigger you into doing same.

Warren Buffet once said, "If you buy things you don't need, soon you will have to sell the things you need". Buying impulsively affects your income negatively. It makes you spend against your initial budget and thwart financial goals already set. This act also gets one into debt. I could remember how a young woman who went shopping was telling her friend that she wants to buy a particular dress because another lady was putting it on. What do you expect if such lady's spending plan was never drafted to accommodate that dress? She will use the money for other things to satisfy her impulsive need.

Impulsive buying causes you to make poor buying decisions. Most times, we end up buying things we really do not need. At this point, we are filled with regrets but the deed has been done. You need to understand that you don't make buying decisions based on how much people use a particular product. Do not succumb to the temptation to buy impulsively.

ALLOWING YOUR EXPENSES OUTRUN YOUR INCOME

One habit you will find among young entrepreneurs is living above their income. It is sad to see people spend more than they earn. In fact, they are always anticipating the month's paycheque barely few days into the month.

The mistake of spending against your income is a deadly habit that can lead one into depression. In cases where you fail to check your income, you will run into debts. This must be corrected if you want to avoid financial crisis. To achieve this, seek to increase your income and reduce your expenses. If possible, reach out for financial guidance and stick to instructions. Do not allow your money control you. Be in charge of your money.

LACK OF EMERGENCY SAVINGS

A man came home from work one day and found his little daughter ill. He had just completed a business deal and had put in all his funds to the deal expecting that it will bring a huge profit. Now, he is neck-hooked. There is nothing that throws one into turmoil like facing an emergency situation and having no funds at hand. This is why you must have an emergency savings account. It helps you keep on in emergency situations until you get working on improving your income source.

To stay out of financial and emotional crisis, you must have emergency savings which can be accessible only during emergency cases. You must learn to allocate a particular amount of money to that account if possible, three months' worth of salary and ensure that it is topped up regularly.

LENDING YOUR MONEY RECKLESSLY

Another mistake people make is lending money without considering how financial literate the borrower is. There is this urge to help people hence, the habit of lending money. However, it is important to note that you do not lend money to a financial illiterate individual and expect them to pay you back. This is a debt that may not be repaid. More advisable, when such person come to you for money, give an amount you can forfeit when he fails to show up. This will save you unnecessary headache.

HAVING ONE SOURCE OF INCOME

One biggest mistake people make these days is limiting their income flow to one source. This is wrong considering the fact that most people who have built wealth actually have more than one source of income. The reason most people do not take this serious is because they feel comfortable in their 9-5 job. They fail to think about the future. What if something happens and warrants that they get laid off from the job? What would be their next move? You might say that you have enough savings until you get another job. What if there was a delay?

LIVING ABOVE YOUR MEANS

Jane is one woman we see a picture of this mistake in. She was spending more than what she got. Little wonder why she goes broke few days after receiving a paycheque. We cannot deny the fact that a lot of people are also guilty of this. How can you be spending above your means? How can you buy things that cost above your income?

The problem is that most persons like to appear above their means. They want people to think that they are living the best of life. They compare themselves with others and try to play and act big against their income. So sad because they end up trying to please the crowd and get what others have at all cost without checking the harm such action brings.

One secret to becoming financially free is living within your means. Oftentimes, we get emotionally down when we do not have what every other person has. This will only cause you to have piles of bills waiting for you. Learn to spend less and within your means. Learn to appreciate what you have and enjoy maximum financial freedom. You will save yourself financial heartbreak.

WORKING HARD AND NOT SMART

With the advent of smart money making opportunities, it is easy to make money without leaving your room. This is a goldmine which most people do not know. This is why many people are working so hard to foot their bills. My regret is that they do not earn full worth of the energy spent.

Hard work alone in any entrepreneurial journey has been defeated in this age. It is no longer how hard you work but how smart. If you do not leverage the countless opportunities to play a big money game, you might remain where you are. I shake my head when I see young people running under the hot sun in pursuit of peanuts. I wish they know that they can utilize that time, think smart, do the right networking and earn massively. This is just like deciding to learn and master a skill, position yourself properly on social media and get hired by those who need you. If you do this right, you will earn exceedingly every month.

ZERO CASH FLOW MANAGEMENT

Earning money is one thing and having that money bring in returns is another thing. With the sublime economic system on board, it is easy to have money in your hand now and have it leave in the next second. Lack of knowledge about cash flow can have you struggle in the new economy.

Also, the way money flows is highly restricted with the huge monetary policies coming almost daily and with the high tax placed on small-scale businesses. As a start-up, you must learn to manage your cash well irrespective of how much it keeps coming your way. This is usually so at the beginning of any business. If you do not pay adequate attention to your cash flow, you will end up back to square one.

PLACING MUCH VALUE ON MONEY THAN ON FAMILY

I attended an event some years back which taught me a lifelong lesson. There was a family of four; a man, wife and two kids, occupying a VIP table at the left corner of the hall. The man was so engrossed in his phone that evening while his wife was also focused on her phone. The kids looked on and saw another family having a hearty chat with each other. From the look on their faces, they were sad.

I need not tell you that those kids will grow with such programmed mindset and would eventually lose track of great relationships. This is the picture of the century. It is not rare to see individuals fixed on their devices with little or no time for their loved ones. I understand that you want to make money at all cost but this should not be to the detriment of your family and friends. That device will not be there for you when you need care and comfort. It is your loved ones who will hold you through any difficult moment.

Cut that gap today by spending time with your loved ones. Do not bring in money matters when it is supposed to be a hearty-chat time. Do not get hooked in the ever busy schedule that you do not reach out to them. Create time for them, have a healthy talk, and share your problems. Who knows if the solution to that problem is lurking in their minds? Research proves that healthy time spent with loved ones boost the healthy state of any individual.

In the next chapter, we will get to know smart money rules we can work with to boost our finance.

CHAPTER 7

MONEY RULES

Jane looked at her image in the mirror. She wasn't seeing that beautiful face that lets out alluring dimples each time she smiled. "This wasn't the image I saw when I visited United Kingdom." She said almost sobbing as memories of her trip to the United Kingdom filled her mind. Her last vacation was in Loughborough in Leicestershire. She could remember how she was snapped into the scintillating view from her exclusive room on the third floor of the hotel. "Indeed, nature is blessed." She had thought and smiled wryly. Her supposed next point of call for vacation this year was Costa del Sol.

Last vacation was one of her best. She had the best of experience during her trip and was determined to spend the next vacation with the girls, but she doubts the possibility. Come to think of it, they have a girls' hangout for that weekend but Jane was checking out excuses not to attend. She wanted to be out of engagements that would have them talk about the next vacation, the next shopping spree, or the next party in town.

"I want to change my financial habit." She said looking so forlorn. She had confided in Deola, her account officer during her meeting with her and she had promised to help her tackle her money problems. Deola did not fail to expose her to some rules she can start working with while they sort things out with regards to the company's cash flow.

"You don't need to panic, Ma'am. I understand how you feel and trust me when I say that you will come out of this unscathed. You need to speak with a finance consultant and expert. I know your company's financial team may have someone knowledgeable in this but you need an external person." Deola said convincingly.

As a serial entrepreneur, I have come to understand that most things we do when it comes to the issue of money are based on what we know and what we do not know. Sadly enough, financial crisis is a respecter of no excuse. I could remember the story of a lady who bought a cloth of nearly 50% of her monthly salary. To her, that was all she needed at that time. It was sad to know that she had other needs at that point but she deemed it wiser to spend such amount on a dress. I may not know the reason but I guess it isn't farfetched from trying to be among the 'happening babes' in town. I got interested in the story of this young woman because she had been searching for a job three years prior to her getting her recent job and when it was time to save, she spent it on irrelevant things. It was obvious that she would run into financial crisis soon.

One rule of spending that you should imbibe is, "Before you spend on anything, calculate the amount of the item by how many hours it took you to make that particular amount. Then ask yourself if the item in question is really worth that long hour of work".

Let's take the lady who bought a cloth worth 50% of her monthly earnings. If she works Monday to Friday 9-5, that means that she works 176 hours every month. If her salary was $220, it means that she bought the dress for $110 which is the pay for 88 hours. 88 hours divided by 8 hours which she works daily will give us 11 days. This means that she worked 11 days to buy a dress that wouldn't add to her income. Weird, right? I didn't add other expenses like logistics and transport fare to and fro her work place. *laughs* This should bring her financial state to a drastic level. At the end of the day, she won't save anything as she is yet to attend to her basic need and her money is little above half her salary.

It is very difficult to ascertain how much money we have made in our entire lifetime. The bigger problem is that out of all we make, we cannot boast of a reasonable amount of money as savings. This is caused by lack of knowledge of money rules or negligence to money rules. The rules of money can be adjusted to fit the 21st-century business and allow for smarter ways to make more money, build wealth, and ensure sustainability. In case you do not know, sustainability is the key to financial freedom.

RULE 1: DESIRE LESS

Do you want to get the world at the snap of your fingers? This is one reason you need to have rule number one in mind. Making money takes time than spending it. It is inconsiderate to work thousands of hours and end up flushing all income made into getting a car, going on a vacation, or buying that thing that wouldn't bring you money. Common sense should tell you that it is wrong. If you want to build a fortune, you should learn to desire less. Give up buying that luxury car or going on that vacation that requires you to empty your bank account. Be in control of your desires. If you want to grow your income, desire less.

RULE 2: KNOW HOW THE ECONOMY WORKS

Having a subtle knowledge of how the economy works will help you know when to invest your money or not especially if you are into stocks. Do you know when the interest rates go up and when it goes down? Can you guess when inflation will hit the market cycle? Can you predict the government's next monetary policy? I have seen entrepreneurs run into financial crisis because they were hit by a policy they could predict but didn't because they lack knowledge of how the economy works. This is why I advise entrepreneurs and individuals who want to be financially free to always read books on money and dailies. Try to speak with your finance consultant and know the best step when there is a change in the interest rate. When such issues come up, you wouldn't be caught unawares.

RULE 3: AVOID PERSONAL DEBT

Borrowing money is not free; I want you to know this before we go on. Taking on debts is not wrong either. However, before deciding to take a loan, you must place emphasis on the gains you expect from it. For instance, you can take a loan to start/grow a business or invest into a viable deal. That notwithstanding, be careful about taking on debts. Never borrow money to buy a car, electronics, or anything else that goes down in value.

RULE 4: SAVE AS MUCH AS YOU CAN

To be financially free, desire less, know how the economy works, avoid debts, and of course, save. You do not envision a future that gives you leverage in cases of financial crisis when you do not save. Saving a specific amount of money is the way to go. This can be done intentionally on weekly, bi-weekly, or monthly basis. You can have a smart saving strategy based on your earning, personality, and even knowledge. The better you know about savings, the more money you have as personal finance. Your location also determines your savings strategy. Paying rent or buying a house, which is more expensive? This will help you plan right. The smart thing about saving is that you can grab investment opportunities each time you spot any.

RULE 5: HAVE A SHORT-TERM STRATEGY

If you love to work with long-term investment, there is a need to have a short-term strategy that can bring you money. Of course, the long term investment plan does not bring you money anytime soon. The smart thing to do is to have a skill or a venture that can bring you daily income. By now, you should know that more skills mean more money. This is why you must invest in personal development. Create and control multiple streams of income so that you can fall back to others when one fails to provide you with enough money.

RULE 6: SPEND LESS THAN YOU EARN

Paying yourself and saving for rainy days is possible only when you spend less than you earn. The easiest way to do this is by sticking to a budget. When you work for a pay, don't get so excited on the day you receive your pay that you forget to spend with your brain. Stick to your budget. A budget allows you to spend tactfully and decide what takes your money or not. I talked about watching your emotion and lifestyle as a financially-wise person. Don't spend more than you earn. In fact, don't spend more than 50% of your income on something that won't bring you money. This is one rule you should have in mind if you want to live a financial-crisis-free life.

RULE 7: STOP WASTING TIME

It is normal to see an average youth chatting and whiling away his time when he would have comfortable made good money if that time was utilized. Time is money and this is why you must use your time judiciously. I know a young woman who works, studies, and also attends to her family duties. She maximizes her 24 hours and ensures that each hour yields something profitable. Today, she has multiple streams of income and all spheres of her life are growing and have recorded positive results. Unproductivity is often as a result of lack of conscious time management. The reason most people are broke is that they do not know that the time they spend on irrelevances can be converted to money. Do not feel that you do not have time and fail to seek ways to earn more money. Even if it is that three hours you use to chat around, direct it into doing something profitable especially now that technology has made learning anything easier.

RULE 8: AVOID HIGH-INTEREST DEBT

It is normal to seek a loan when you want to start a business. For me, I do not advise you get a loan as a small-scale entrepreneur. Loans are favourable when business owners and investors take it.

However, if you must get a loan, ensure that the interest rate is clearly spelt out. If the interest rate is high, avoid such loan. You might be tricked into accepting such loan; have you thought about the risk of deficient returns? How would you pay up if the expectations you envisioned were not met. As a money-oriented individual, you need to think smart. It is better not to take a loan if the interest rate is on the high side than end up paying back with the proceeds of the business for which you sought the loan in the first place.

RULE 9: PAY YOURSELF FIRST

One routine I have adopted over the years is to pay myself after completing a project or receiving a pay for a job or service rendered. This implies that you pay a certain amount of money to a separate account. That account is solely for savings. This is one rule you need to take to heart. This is an old rule of thumb that helps you save, rather than spending all your money. Even if your budget is tight, as soon as you get paid, put some money into savings. Saving first, rather than last, means you are much more likely to save money instead of spending it.

RULE 10: TALK ABOUT MONEY. BE HONEST ABOUT IT

Talking about money has become a sin to most people. When people see you talk about money, they wonder if you are self-contended. Most people have been conditioned to keep mute each time the issue of money is discussed. They want financial security but are afraid of kicking off a conversation that will help them achieve it. Not talking about your money problems can hurt those around you especially when the other party ought to know what's up with your financial life. The more you talk about money, the more open you are and the more better your life becomes. Even relationships where money issues are openly tackled are known to have recorded huge success.

Couples should talk about money. This is largely evident in how a family is thrown into confusion when the breadwinner dies. When couple fail to talk about money issues, how then is the issue of will and inheritance tackled? A man who dies without a will leaves his family at the mercy of his extended family who confiscate his property. It is high time couples started having salient discussions on money. With this step, families are protected from external struggles for inheritance evident in most African homes.

Also, take stock of the family's finance. If you are about getting married, this should be discussed at the pre-marital stage. Know the financial capability of your spouse. State your expectations and agree on how the family expenses would be tackled. Most people ignore this with the thought of "There is a man who would oversee all the expenses" while the man might be thinking "She is earning, I am sure she would contribute". In a situation where there is such disparity in mindset and view probably because they came from different background and had disparate views about family finance, there is high tendency that such could bring about issues in the marriage.

"When couples fail to talk about money, it could result to something similar to the case of a man and his wife who operate a joint account. When the man was having financial issues in his place of work, he didn't mention it to his wife. At a point, the woman felt betrayed seeing that the rate of savings from the side of the man was low." Deola said and smiled after drawing that analogy. She loved the way Jane was taking note of the points she had mentioned. Jane, on the other hand, remembered her friend, Brenda. Brenda had told the girls how her husband always wanted her to foot some of the bills at home. "That is an unscrupulous thought. Daniel is the man for crying out loud. Why would he expect me to sort out his responsibilities?" She said, trying too hard to steady her nerves. The girls looked at her, surprised. Jane was more confused. Back home, her mum who was a civil servant settled some of the bills without waiting for her husband. Here was Brenda complaining that she couldn't do same. "Yes! Our background really affects our attitude towards money," She explained to Deola who interrupted her thoughts by asking if she understood her.

Daniel, Brenda's husband was of the belief that both husband and wife should contribute to the upkeep of the home. His parents did. "Why was Brenda acting indifferent towards the issue?" He thought. This is why both parties need to be free when it comes to the issue of money. If you both would run a joint account and share the household bills, talk about it; before marriage preferably. It is vital to avoid money mistakes that could hamper the smooth running of the home. Talk about money with your partner, your family members, and everyone close to you. Sometimes, creating a clear picture of your financial state and getting them in perspective of what is happening would be a relief to the seeming financial needs they might be expecting from you.

RULE 11: INCREASE YOUR SAVING EACH TIME YOU GET A PAY RAISE

It is usual to see people raise their lifestyle when they get a raise in salary. This is not wise. If your salary has always funded your lifestyle and you are contented with it, don't move significantly above that. When you get a raise in salary, put it into savings rather than spending it. This keeps you and your lifestyle in check.

RULE 12: CHANGE DON'T REPAIR

It is most likely to want to repair faulty appliances but the truth is that you need to weigh the pros and cons. When an appliance is faulty, it is advisable to buy a new one especially if the appliance is over a decade old or if the cost of repair is half the original cost. It is better to replace such appliance as repairing them might lead to subsequent issues with the other parts.

RULE 13: WINDFALLS SHOULD BE INVESTED

It is exciting to get money which you never expected. It could be a gift, a bonus from your work place, a 13th month pay, a cash win, or even a sort of inheritance. Do not be tempted to spend all. Save more of it and spend just 3%. Don't get swept away by the ecstasy of such money that you fail to come up with a smart way to spend such money.

RULE 14: HAVE A SMART BUDGET QUOTA

Having a smart budget quota saves you from a lot of troubles. If you're new to budgeting, try using the 50-30-20 quota. This is how it works: 50% of your pay towards necessities (food, shelter, utilities, clothing, etc.), 30% towards lifestyle choices (vacations, gym fees, hobbies, cell-phone plans, etc.), and 20% towards financial goals and priorities (extra debt payments, savings, etc.). If you are receiving salary, as soon as your pay comes, divide the money and send to the allocated account. This isn't a perfect budget plan, but you can get effective result with this.

RULE 15: IDENTIFY YOUR BUDGET LEAKS

A lot of people end up experiencing financial crisis even after setting up a budget. The problem is that there are a lot of budget leaks yet unidentified. When you tend to spend above your stated budget, the best thing is to track your spending. You can either go for the less way of tracking expenses which is taking note of those areas where you tend to over-spend. They are your budget leaks. These areas could include clothings, gadgets, outings, etc. Identifying these areas and tracking your expenses help you keep track of how you spend your money without getting confused by an over-detailed checklist.

RULE 16: HAVE AN EMERGENCY FUND

Rainy days are bound to show up. Emergencies happen. One might fall sick or there might be a breakdown of gadgets or even the car. It is usual to have people beg in such cases of emergency. This is why you should always be prepared. Have an emergency fund account. Put in part of your income in a high-yield savings account. The money there is to attend to unforeseen circumstances. Such funds are usually used in cases of life and death. The rule is to save three to six months' expenses in an emergency fund. If you doubt the security of your job, it is advised that you save eight to ten months' worth of expenses. Remember, you are saving an estimate of your monthly expenses and not income.

RULE 17: TRY THE 72% RULE WHEN INVESTING

There are a lot of investment rules you can work with. One of them is the 72% rule. Use the rule of 72 to determine how long it will take your investment to double. To use this rule, divide 72 by the expected growth rate of your investments, expressed as a percentage. If you expect to earn 10% per year, for instance, it'll take you about 7.2 years to double your money.

RULE 19: HAVE A TRACK RECORD OF YOUR FINANCIAL GROWTH

Track your financial growth. Have a checklist for determining how much better your portfolio is. This should be done at least every five years. It helps you know if your investments are growing. Check your net worth annually. It helps you identify leaks in your money streams. When you notice any, consider rebalancing your investments.

RULE 20: PAY FROM THE HIGH TO THE LOW

When you are stuck with debts, one easy way to come off those debts is by paying off the ones with the high-interest rate first. There are a lot of debt repayment methods but trust me when I say that the best and convenient method is this. You might want to increase your income and avert the urge to pay the debts with high-interest rate but trust me, those debts will linger on. Wouldn't it be better that you gradually pay them off and become debt free?

RULE 21: START SAVING FOR RETIREMENT TODAY

It is advisable to save for retirement. Do not allow yourself to be entangled in the troubles of retiring and having insufficient funds to live the best of life. Save 10–20% of your income for retirement. If your income increases, you can increase your savings rate to 30%. Use your current expenses rate to calculate your retirement needs. An easy way to calculate this is by checking if you have saved 1x your annual salary by the time you are 35, 2x by 40, 3x by 45, etc. This will help you know if you will have enough when you retire. The deal is to be ready for retirement.

RULE 22: NEVER GO INTO DEBTS FOR DEPRECIATING ASSETS

It is easy to get a loan but it is the most stinging act when you fail to pay up. This is why you shouldn't go into debts for assets that do not appreciate. I talked about a young man who bought a car with his money and ended up being an ex to money. Now, let's narrow it to getting a loan to buy a car. A car is one of the depreciating assets you can ever take a loan to acquire because its value depreciates by the day. Do not buy a car on loan. Pay cash.

Before you take that loan or go into debt for any asset, check if your net worth for that asset will increase monthly if you buy them. If no, do not take the loan.

Deola concluded and assured her of connecting her with a well-known finance consultant by name Abidemi Josh. With this, Jane was seriously anticipating her appointment with him. She had surfed the net that night and found clips of his appearance on TV and highlights of some of his speaking gigs. He looked young and smart with all the awards and achievements his brand had received so far. That night, she slept, hoping that a new scene would play out in her financial life soon.

PHASE 3

THE NEW GAME

CHAPTER 8

PLAYING THE MONEY GAME THE NEW WAY

Jane had a meeting fixed with the finance consultant at 10 that Thursday morning. It has been a whole hell of week calculating; adding and subtracting. It was becoming clear to her that she needed to work on the modes of her money game if she really wanted to get off this crisis anytime soon. As she made her way into Standard Invest Co. that morning, her breath started flopping. She began feeling unsure of what she really wanted to tell him.

She got to know of Abidemi during her last discussion with her account manager, Deola. Jane had poured her heart to her and asked that she directed her to someone who could help her out of the quagmire she had found herself and company in. After sharing some money rules with her, Deola ensured that she kept track of Jane's income and advised her where necessary. When Abidemi sent her a message accepting her request for her client to meet with him, she called Jane and broke the news to her.

"He requests to see you at 10 am Thursday. Please ensure you open up to him. He is quite a busy but accommodating fellow and I am sure he will help you out in his own way." She said. Jane was confused and pensive as she waited to be ushered into his office. He was indeed a busy man. "He looks quite young. He should be in his early thirties," she thought and went further and greeted him. His face was fixed to a fold of papers on his desk when she walked in. He looked up with a smile and offered her a seat. He introduced himself and quickly briefed her on what Deola had told him about her. As first, it was a cessational conversation until Abidemi took over. He understood that Jane's problem was that she was playing the money game the old way and he was committed to holding her through getting it right.

Money is a game and like every typical game, one needs clear knowledge of the rules. It was time to apply those rules but first, she needed to understand the game. In her case, money has been a game played with the old mentality. However, the smart ones are playing it with the new mentality. The game of money can only be won if you know what those who play it right know. In this chapter, I will be showing you some key factors Abidemi shared with Jane which you can leverage to be on top of the money game.

KNOW YOUR WHY

It is easy to hear people say that they want to make money. When I get to mentor youth aging 18-35, I hear them tell tales of what they will use the millions and billions they want to make for. It is your WHY that will tell if you will really make that money and how you will make it. Knowing your WHY is paramount for everyone who wants to launch a life of financial freedom. A man whose reason for making money is to buy a car will feel satisfied when he gets that amount of money for the car. However, the man whose reason for making money is to build sustainable wealth will make more money because he has wealth consciousness.

What drives an individual determines the extent to which he/she will go. This applies to money. To play the money game the right way, have a strong WHY. Know why you need to make money. Is it to be famous or to possess power or even to carry out philanthropic gestures? Is it to change the financial state of your family for good? Maybe you are someone who got frustrated and mocked while growing up; do you wish to prove that you too can make money? You need a strong WHY if you must make money.

It is your WHY that will push you to wake up every day while making you come up with strategies to increase your income. It is your WHY that will keep you going even when you fail in a business. Your WHY will determine if you will become a business owner, investor, self-employed, or employee. More reasons you should know the model to employ when building wealth. Of course, not all models will work for you.

Your WHY will, to an extent, drive your enthusiasm to make money. Someone's goal might be to make $1,000 dollars and another might be to make $10,000 dollars. If you are the latter, your drive to make money will be higher than the former. If you are someone who hopes to have a retirement savings of $10,000, your WHY is stronger than the person who wants to have $5,000 in his/her retirement plan. The fact here is that everyone is satisfied as far as they were able to meet their target.

For you to play the money game right, you must have a passionate WHY that is compelling enough to push you into taking action. When it seems as though things are not going the planned way, you will need a strong WHY to fall back to. You will need a conviction that is capable of keeping you on track.

HAVE INVESTMENT GOALS

When you discover your WHY, it is important to direct same question to investing. Ask yourself, "Why am I investing?" The reply to this question will tell which investment would suit you. If you are a married man with family, bills to foot, and rent to pay, going into the stock market with all your funds is like shooting yourself in the foot. Stocks are volatile and are often of great value on the long run. It will be advisable to go for less volatile investments like treasury bills and mutual funds. However, if you are saving to start a project in five years time, you can opt for the stock market

Remember that your investment could be different from another persons'. While you are investing to buy a car, or buy landed assets, another person might be investing for retirement purposes. Like I mentioned earlier, someone's goal might be to make $5,000 dollars and another might be to make $10,000 dollars. If you are the latter, your drive to make money will be higher than the former. Hence, your investment goal will tell which investment would be preferable for you.

THINK BIG. THINK POSSIBILITY

The mind, just like we mentioned in chapter two of this book, is the basic repertoire of all you hear and accept. Anything you do is greatly affected by what your mind knows and thinks at the moment. The state of living and the level of progress in our lives is determined by the state of our thoughts. Knowing that our successes are first approved by the mind, we need to ensure that what we think and conceive in our thoughts is synonymous to what we hope to achieve. If you think negativity, you will always get negative results in your money game and vice versa.

A step ahead of what every other person knows is leverage especially in the money game. More reason you need to constantly feed your mind with what is required of you to always top the money game. Think versatile and learn new things every day. Open your mind to innovations and go with the tide. Do not get stuck in mediocrity by ignoring salient opportunities to become better and boost your knowledge and income stream. See the Internet as a school and a market by learning and selling there.

Believe that you can get results from anything you do. Do not get swept away by the many talks filtering the space. Know what works for you and stick to it. Train your mind to see possibility always. Coming to the idea of using the Internet right, there are a lot of money-making opportunities there. You should check them out.

KILL THAT FEAR

The predominant factor holding individuals from doing well in the money game is the fear of 'what may happen'. There are a lot of reasons to live in fear especially with the heightened attention drawn to it by the happenings in the society. We hear stories of investment schemes crashing, businesses running into debts, and self-employed individuals giving up on their vision. When it comes to the issue of money, people's fear are heightened. Little wonder it is difficult to convince a layman to invest his hard-earned money.

If you want to play a better game when it comes to money, you need to face your fears. You cannot take salient decisions if the fear in you controls you. You must move beyond the frightening noise and take actionable steps to boost your financial life even when it seems a risk. After all, making money in itself is risky. Take that bold step. Do not be left behind in the money journey. You do not want to look on as others cast their nets in the ocean of financial stability while you look on cheering them up. They never got there with the fear in them. They ignored all odds to ensure a better future for themselves and generation yet unborn. Be a part of the success team. Kill that fear.

BE OPEN TO INNOVATION

This is the era of Internet and Technology and trust me when I say that people are boosting their income stream by leveraging the Internet. Today, Artificial Intelligence is also taking over. Haven't you seen the report that says that robots will be replacing a good number of employees soon? This is the extent to which innovation has brought us. But you wouldn't want to be caught unawares right?. This is why you must begin to think and act innovatively.

The goal of every man is to build wealth that will be sustainable. Creating such wealth shouldn't be tied to you showing up every day. Do you know that there are people who earn billions of naira from their homes? Do you know that there are people who run automated businesses that bring them money even while they are asleep? My company has launched her trading currency; Kwatcoin, and smart individuals are investing and earning in cashless mode. Multi-billion naira businesses are offering dependable services even without physical locations. People who take steps to start and run such businesses are not low thinkers. They are innovatives who go with the tides.

The difference between two men who have a business idea is the level of innovative thinking applied to it. Smart people know that they cannot run their businesses the old way and expect to play the money game the new way. Instead, they do the old thing using the new and innovative process. They have taken a leap in their money game and to keep abreast of the growth, they think and dream big. Winning the money game in the 21st century isn't a child's play and it is won by those who go extra miles to make things work in their favour. You cannot think small to attain such level.

TAKE THE STEPS GRADUALLY

If you hear people share their stories and the steps they took to build their businesses to the stage it is, you will see reasons to take that step gradually. Don't try to start from a level that would weigh you down both financially and emotionally. It could be that smartphone you have or that skill you have; start with it. Don't wait for when you will find bigger opportunities. Leverage the little ones in view.

Come up with smart ideas and apply your knowledge to make it work. Don't give excuses of little capital when you can start something with it. Anything is possible in this era. I have seen people who started their businesses with their social media handles and today, they are doing well. You too can build a sustainable income stream when you learn to take gradual steps using that thing you have at the moment.

BE UNCOMFORTABLE WITH MEDIOCRITY

Using what you have now does not mean that you should feel comfortable using it forever. Getting satisfied by what you have at hand or what you are able to access at the moment is a clear description of mediocrity. You cannot make money if you are satisfied with the way it was done in times past. This is more reason you need to have an inventive and innovative mindset. If it requires you to work your ass all day to make a specific amount of money, you should consider coming up with ways to make that same amount of money in few hours. The easiest way to do this is by applying technological knowledge around that initial idea. You cannot do this if you are satisfied with the state of affairs in which you find yourself in. The deal is to have you think hard and forge deep into the world of knowledge and apply that knowledge to your money game.

BE FINANCIALLY EDUCATED

Money isn't taught in schools. Maybe it is more reason those who think they got the academic qualification still find themselves meshed in financial crisis. We exist in a society that gives access to those with competitive edge. To stay abreast of the money game, you need to be financially educated. Financial literacy is what guarantees financial independence and trust me when I say that it beats the normal education.

This is not to say that going to school is not worth it. Of course it is, but it is not a benchmark for financial freedom. It is your desire to learn more about money and wealth that will assure you a place at the top of the money game. Learn to improve your income. Work on building multiple streams of income. Master the principles of the money game and play it right. Remember, no one cares about your financial state hence, you need to be in charge. Don't think that anyone will offer you a pot of money. Instead of waiting for one, learn how to fill your money pot and never allow it go into lack.

CREATE MONEY GOALS AND STICK TO THEM

It is not about creating goals but sticking to them. Successful people are committed to their goals. They have money goals and ensure they stick to these goals. They are accountable to their goals. If you want to build a net worth of ten million dollars in three years, you must have daily, weekly, monthly, and yearly goals with benchmarks to help you actualize that main goal. Saying 'I want to make so-so amount of money' is not the deal. Be clear on your goals. It will help you focus your mind on things that are of great importance. The deal is to stick to that goal and achieve it. You can get equipped by looking out for books and courses on wealth creation.

While you take action towards that goal, ensure you are accountable. Avoid procrastination. Most times, it is not that we lack knowledge of what to do but that we leave all we should do for the next hour, day or month. The more you procrastinate, the more you allow time pass away. Most times, you end up not doing that thing. The deal is to do it now!

BE FINANCIALLY SMART AND INTELLIGENT

What determines how much money you will make in your lifetime is how smart you are when the issue of money is brought up. Being able to take financial decisions at the right time and be in charge of the result is what keeps you at the top of your money game as a smart investor. This is a spectacular feature in financially-smart individuals.

Financial intelligence is attained when you take succinct stance on issues relating to finance in such a way that allows for proper reasoning, clarification of options, and opting for the best option. This allows for avoidance of many money mistakes in your money game. When you prove to be financially intelligent, you find yourself taking money decisions without fear of financial crisis in the long run

However, when you are financially smart and intelligent, you need no soothsayer to tell you how much of your money goals you will be crushing and how much better you will be playing the money game.

In the next chapter, we will see how Jane took up investment schemes that helped her build a smart financial life. What else did Abidemi offer her?

CHAPTER 9

THE SMART MONEY INVESTOR

Things were now getting clearer as Abidemi explained to Jane what she needed to up her money game. At a point, she looked at him and thought, "What a smart young man". She kept on noting all that he said. She was committed to playing smart this time around. Her countenance was brightened as soon as he asked her if she was ready to play the money game right. Her smiles said it all.

Abidemi was a high-profile investment consultant who had worked with a good number of banks since his graduation from Harvard University. He was such a compendium of financial intelligence. In three years, he has gone from working with banks to building his financial agency. His clients include CEOs and managers of high-worth companies. As he spoke to Jane, all that ran through her mind was 'This man is good!'

He wanted her to think away from just her company's funds to her personal funds. "It is not enough to boost your company's funds. If we fail to work on your personal funds, you will fall back to square one," he advised. "I want you to build a strong financial personal portfolio. This is not about what your company earns but your net worth." He added.

There is no agreed approach to investing. Everyone has disparities when it comes to earning potential, risk profile, and financial obligation. This was Jane's problem. Despite running a company with net worth of millions of naira and receiving a monthly income of over eight hundred thousand naira, she lacked knowledge of investment strategies for her personal income.

"What is your investment strategy?" Abidemi asked. She was lost. This was that moment when she had to be cleared on how to go about her financial security. "I really need guidelines on this now." She said with hopes. "I see," he smiled. "You can build an income portfolio and asset allocation system by investing in diversified long

-term. This way, you will have more than one asset class and have a stated proportion of income that will go into each." He said and showed her a number of asset classes she could invest in.

STOCK MARKET

When it comes to the issue of stocks, a lot of people shy away from it. To them, it is such a risky asset class. It is true that the level of risk in stocks is high but one can still leverage this market to build financial freedom. The stock market is becoming investment friendly with the checks now carried out on companies selling their stocks.

However, due to the increasing devaluation of money, it is preferable to invest in stocks for long term because they are volatile. They increase in value in the long run. But you need to tread cautiously when investing in the stock market. The stock market isn't one you come into with a short-term plan. You might be shooting yourself in the foot.

Do you remember Fred; the one who became an ex to money? He began to pick the pieces of his life. He sought financial knowledge and equipped himself with the necessary information after getting a job with a multi-national company. He was paid three hundred thousand naira monthly. His friend, Greg, was also paid same amount. Due to his experience as an ex to money *smiles*, he was very careful about how he spends. He started saving 50% of his monthly salary. By six months, he was able to buy some stocks. In less than two months, the price of the stock rose by 18% and that was a win for him. He shared this news with his friend, Greg, who decided to also invest in the stock market. Long story short, Greg put his all his savings into stocks and the prices crashed. He was at the losing end as he needed the money to sort out family expenses.

People make the mistake of going into an investment because someone they know did. They fail to come to terms with the knowledge that is needed to make such investment. It is sad because little or no attention is paid to their earning potential, risk profile, and financial obligation. Greg forgot that he was a married man with three kids and a wife who was doing nothing for a living. Fred, on the other hand, had a career woman as a wife, so it was convenient to invest into stocks after consulting with his wife. She was also contributing to the family income so they had nothing to worry about.

Fred and Greg may be earning the same salary but their income sustainability mode is convoluted. Fred has lesser financial obligations to meet compared to Greg who pays the rent, stocks the grocery store, pays the utility bills, sees to the children's school fees, and foots emergency bills all alone! So, Greg actually shot himself in the foot. Fred was investing into stock on long-term basis and the longer the stocks stay, the higher the value and interest on return.

Stocks are volatile in nature but they rise in value when bought on long-term basis. When investing in stocks, ensure you understand financial reports and draw a clue from the numbers presented. Know when the numbers are falling and buy stocks, and sell only when it is rising. This way, your money value is increased. Work with a team of smart brokers and analysts who understand how the market works.

One key strategy you should work with is this, "Do not buy stocks when everyone is rushing to buy". Work with market insurance strategies like margins, short selling, stock calls etc. Ensure that insider behaviour like corporate governance, matrix, and share ownership are maximised. Finally, buy companies with strong patent, monopoly, and are run with strong monetary policy. Remember, do not sell stocks when the prices fall but buy at this point. Of course, they will be sold at giveaway prices.

REAL ESTATE

This is the booming business in the economy at the moment and trust me when I say that smart people who understand it as a long term investment with minimum risk and succinct cash flow are finding their way into the sector. For real estate, there is an expectation of constant increase in value especially in developed cities and towns.

However, buying a house is not real estate investment. This is supported by the saying that "If the net cash flow from an asset is not positive, then it is a liability". A good example of Real Estate Investment is buying lands and property at discounted prices from developing areas. This way, you can lease it to farmers or skilled entrepreneurs who need open space for their businesses.

When going into real estate, decide which strategy would suit you best. Would you go for a property flipper or a holder? At best, being a developer is a more profitable strategy. You can build a portfolio that allows you earn consistently from the industry. This was why Wisdom Kwati City project was birthed.

The Wisdom Kwati City is a platform where real estate investors who do not have the knowledge or idea of how to invest their money are held through smart ways to do so. They invest with us to build a house for them which they can rent to other people. As an investor, you get to pay for only two years of the mortgage while you have 13 years to balance the rest. This means that by the third year, you can have someone rent the house and service the mortgage while you make your profit.

People do not necessarily have to go through the task of buying lands because they want to invest in real estate. Most times, these people get duped because they do not know about engineering techniques, cost, and building itinerary. Now, crude 'professionals' leverage their ignorance to dupe them of their hard-earned money. For this reason and more, we now come up as a trusted partner for real estate investors.

When investing in Real Estate, invest in developing and quite disturbed areas. This could be areas experiencing famine, war, or incessant robbery attacks. People will want to relocate and sell off their property at discounted prices. Trust me, there won't be unrest in that area forever. Invest in those areas. Strategically buy spaces that can be used to site lock-up stores for rent. Look out for buildings with open spaces at the front and liaise with the owner for you to buy the space. Ensure those buildings are in profit-oriented locations.

One thing you should also bear in mind is that an investment in real estate does not come with stated risks. At a point, property value might dwindle and rise at another point. The deal is to know how to invest in such a way that your investment principal grows in line with your investment.

TREASURY BILLS

According to FMDQ Securities Exchange, treasury bills are short-term sovereign debt securities maturing in one year or less. They are sold at a discount and redeemed at par. These bills are by nature, the most liquid money market securities and are backed by the guarantee of the Federal Government of a nation.

Treasury Bills can be bought through any official dealer. The easiest these days are through banks' treasury bill mobile application. Treasury Bills is sold every other Wednesday (bi-weekly) as announced by the CBN. The CBN announces issuances on their websites and in the pages of national dailies. You can also ask your bank account officer to notify you ahead of an issuance.

To buy Treasury Bills, you will have to approach your bank requesting for a form. You fill the form with your personal information also indicating the amount you want to buy as well as your bid rate. With the advent of banks' treasury bills mobile application, you are only required to fill a signup form once. (Culled from the net)

BONDS

According to the Nigerian Stock Exchange, bonds are fixed income instruments issued by entities to raise funds. The issuer of a bond presents the bond as a promise to make available regular, fixed, income payments to the investor or the buyer of the bond who is also the bondholder. These income payments are known as coupons and bonds which pay coupons twice a year are known as semi-annual coupon bonds.

There are also bonds that make coupon payments annually, known as annual coupon bonds. Bonds which make no coupon payments are called zero coupon bonds, or deep discount bonds. In making a decision to buy a bond, you should consider a number of factors such as the tenure of the bond, the coupon payments expressed as a single percentage rate, and the yield-to-maturity or just simply, yield.

Various bond types include Federal Government Bonds, State/Local Government Bonds, Supranational Bonds, Corporate Bonds, Green Bonds, Eurobounds, etc. (Culled from the net)

MUTUAL FUNDS

Another asset class and investment coordinate you can take up is the mutual fund. Here, funds from investors are used to invest in securities and assets that will bring huge ROI in the long run. These assets could include stocks, bonds, treasury bills, etc. Here, the funds collected are invested with a view of accumulating high-income interest by the fund investors.

There is always a fund management team headed by a manager. The agency is usually a registered financial institution and helps their investors to build financial security by taking up the risk of investment. The good part of this asset class is that you do not need to worry about your money. The Mutual Fund Agency takes professional decisions on your behalf. All you need do is invest and await your money and ROI.

CRYPTOCURRENCY

The most important feature of a cryptocurrency is that it is not controlled by any central authority: the decentralized nature of the blockchain makes cryptocurrencies theoretically immune to the old ways of government control and interference. Cryptocurrencies can be sent directly between two parties via the use of private and public keys. These transfers can be done with minimal processing fees, allowing users to avoid the steep fees charged by traditional financial institutions. This is exactly what one stands to get when they invest in Kwatcoin. Today, cryptocurrencies have become a global phenomenon and smart people are investing in it.

"With this, you have seen how much you can invest and how you can do so without burning yourself." Abidemi said and looked at her. She had this sublime impression that attracted her to him. He knew that most young women in her class often find themselves in this mess of financial crisis because of impulsive spending. Her case isn't any different but he was determined to help sort things out for her.

After her session with Abidemi that morning, she felt a new 'her' was about to be birthed. Her problem wasn't that she didn't know about these things he mentioned but she lacked practical knowledge of applying them. Here she was getting it directly from an MBA holder who has imprinted his foot print in the finance industry. "He looks real good," she fantasised as she made to take her dinner before drawing out her investment strategy as he advised.

CHAPTER 10

MONEY IDEAS TO LEVERAGE IN THE 21ST CENTURY

Jane became a different person after her meeting with Abidemi. She has cut down on spending and was now committed to living a life of financial freedom. Abidemi has been of great help to her. Their conversations have overtime moved from the money talks to some sweet endearing 'gists'. They were to have dinner the next evening and she was seriously anticipating it.

Graneal Foods Ltd was gradually getting off her financial *brouhaha*. They got the contract with Hollisi Limited and Abidemi also put out his time and effort to offer his knowledge. He was a one-time fierce project strategist for one of the consulting firms in Nigeria before starting out his agency. With his help, Jane and her team closed countless deals. She was blessed to have him.

Jane grew from just overseeing the financial growth of the company and the business to using her social media handles to build a strong and influential personal brand. Her weekends were always booked with speaking gigs as she gets invited to speak and inspire people. She became a finance coach and runs a mentoring programme to help a good number of young ladies who desire to start a business but lack steps and knowledge of how to get started. With her experience and wealth of knowledge, she was listed as one of the top 100 women by Leading Ladies Foundation, Africa. She was now earning from what she loves to do; teaching and speaking.

Making money in the 21st century isn't restricted to physical businesses. Today, the social media platforms have become a market for skilled and knowledge-filled individuals. Right on this platform, people are taking steps to productify what they know and build influence that automatically translates to money. The 21st-century business idea can be discussed under passion, experience, skill, hobby, talent, creativity, knowledge, expertise, etc.

There are many avenues to make money in today's society. Opportunities are coming up especially with platforms that allow people to put up their content and showcase their expertise. People land jobs from these platforms and rake in multiple figures as pay. While others spend time doing irrelevant things on social media, you can leverage the platform to show your skill and expertise, and get paid. The deal is to help people with solutions that can increase their net worth.

This isn't some sort of child's play you know. You must commit to learning what works and applying them in your business. This might come right in the time you spend watching movies or scrolling aimlessly through social media newsfeed. You must start doing something, saying something, and providing value in that area for people to come to terms with what you do and stand for.

Karabow as a company has a social media presence but her founder also ensures that he spreads the message of the company and provides information with regards to what the company stands for. My position as a finance consultant gives me an edge in the entrepreneurial world. So you see, establishing authority on the virtual space boils down to you consistently doing one particular thing and getting known for it.

Check yourself for what you can teach. Research on the profitable nature of the niche. Is it what people would pay to learn? Can people invest in that solution you have? You need to find a niche that will bring profit when you give value and not one that will be a one-way affair; you giving and not receiving. Remember that this isn't just about passion but about profitability. While you select a market that suits you, ensure that it is a profitable one.

Don't do what everyone is doing because you see them. Do what works for you. Don't jump from one niche to the other because people are doing well in it. If you fail to do your findings before starting out, you will keep moving from one niche to another. Inasmuch as you are certain about your choice of niche, stick to it and make it work.

Have a platform where you can connect with your audience. Ensure you feed them with knowledge in that niche of yours. Provide them with content that answers the many questions that perturb them. Build a movement of people who understand and believes in what you have to offer. When they know, like, and trust you, they can exchange their money for the knowledge you have. This is something you can do at your spare time each day so you do not necessarily have to quit your job or give up on your business to do this.

Productify your knowledge. Open yourself to training and speaking gigs. Position yourself as an expert by writing a book. Look out for how best to serve your audience and solve their problems. You can host events that will have them come together to share knowledge and learn. You can have virtual courses and consultation sessions where they pay to have your time and your brain.

While you do these, establish trust. With time, everyone begins to see you as an expert and each time something relating to your niche is mentioned, your name becomes the recurring solution provider on their lips. As you do this, you are earning from multiple streams of income. I bet this is the kind of life you will want to live; a life of financial freedom and less stress.

CHAPTER 11

AFTER THIS, WHAT'S NEXT?

Jane walked into KFC that evening. She was wearing a red fitted gown with gold accessories. She looked so beautiful. That wasn't the first time she was having dinner with Abidemi but this time, she was doing so as a woman smashing her money goals. Her face glittered. The last time she was at his place, he asked her what her plans for vacation was. She was mute. She didn't know if he was testing her to know how financially wise she has become. She knew that she was in control now but she needed a vacation like seriously.

What are your plans for vacation?" He asked. "I don't know for now," she tottered and quickly made for the kitchen. "Not too fast!" He stopped her. "You should not be afraid of spending your money. The fact that you are now financially free from debts doesn't mean that you wouldn't give yourself a treat." He smiled as she *shylishly* came back to the sofa. "What if we go to Costa del Sol next month? You know you have always wanted to go there." He quipped. "You are not serious, are you?" She said in creepy-hushed tones. "Of course, I am."

She smiled as memories of that discussion flashed her mind. "Good evening, Ma'am, and welcome to KFC." The waiter had greeted. "Thank you." She had replied with beeming smiles while using her eyes to search for her host. As she caught a glimpse of him, their eyes locked and they smiled. He was dressed in a black designer suit with cream shirt and looked so handsome in it. "You look stunning." He complimented her and ushered her into a seat.

This was her feeling on top of the world. In less than six months, Abidemi had greatly affected her money life. He made her view life from a different and stable perspective. He changed her mindset about money and made her set huge money goals and celebrated her each time she reached any. She hasn't met her billion naira goal but she was already feeling good about herself. She was now in control of her money and was making smart investment decisions already. Her impulsive nature of spending was at its minimum and she wasn't giving into reckless spending anymore. Her financial goals seem achievable and her money streams were consistently bringing her income.

Jane looked at herself in the mirror as she washed her hands after using the restroom. She smiled at the woman she was becoming. A woman who has grown to be a model to young women. A woman who is in control of her money. A woman who has assets in stocks and landed property. A woman who knows that her net worth validates every other aspects of her life including her closet. She was now the woman who understands that wealth isn't about her physical money and the things she could buy for pleasure. Wealth is creating systems that keeps you in check in the long run. Wealth is about tomorrow. She now understands that to become wealthy depends on her decision and today, she is living it. She patted her face and walked back into the restaurant.

She met a scenario and was taken aback. "Please, marry me." Abidemi came on one knee smiling as he looked up to her with a ring in his hand.

USE YOUR WEALTH WISELY

From the beginning of this book, you might be wondering why I was passionate about sharing the knowledge I have here. My analogies, stories, illustrations, trademarked terminologies, and the keys and strategies are a product of experience. I have come to realize that money isn't a theoretical subject matter and the earlier we come to terms with that, the better for us.

We may have at one point or the other been like the old Jane. We might have committed many money mistakes. But the new Jane, our money hero, has overcome those taunting mistakes. She has become one smart, fearless, determined, and money-conscious woman. She has moved from the fear-hampered woman to one who speaks about money in great confidence. She is committed to raising brilliant money-minded individuals like you. She believes that success in life is greatly determined by how much impact one has on others.

It is always said that "The reason most of us aren't rich is that we always spend it all on ourselves." That was my driving force; the zeal to reach out and impact positively on the society. When you use money to make a difference, to have a positive impact, you get the chance to do more. You will also be able to access other opportunities that come with it. Invest in people. Invest in the society. Let your money leave a positive imprint in the sand of your time.

While you are young, use your money wisely. Invest in worthy causes. Do not allow the wind of spendthrift pull you. Most people will earn a fortune during their workable age but if you fail to build wealth and use it wisely, you will end up broke. Even if you start working late in life, you can work and plan for a blissful retirement. The task is entirely up to you to determine where your money will go!

You too can be like Jane, our money hero!

CONCLUSION

In the words of Philip E. Humbert, "Millionaires don't necessarily earn more, but they spend less. They live below their means. They live well, but they do not spend on items that depreciate, or on frivolous items to impress their friends. They invest wisely, often in their own businesses, or in stocks or other investments that they understand and are willing to monitor closely. They take money seriously. And, they expect to retire wealthy. They value money, and they pay attention to it. They manage it. They accumulate and they let it work for them, rather than always working for money, from one paycheque to the next.

Be the next money hero!

ABOUT THE AUTHOR

Wisdom Kwati is a finance consultant and the founder & CEO of Karabow Group; developers of Wisdom Kwati Cities (https://wisdomkwaticity.com) across Nigeria, with expansion-cities projects already in Ghana, South Africa, and Cameroon as of 2020. He also founded the already-under-design famous 1 trillion dollars mega project, Wisdom Kwati Smart City, to be sited on a 157,000 hectares at Ibeju Lekki Lagos state, Nigeria. Wisdom Kwati has closed deals worth billions of dollars and has helped many others as he serves as a business mentor to many business executives, entrepreneurs, leaders, etc.

Recently he founded Africa's first stable cryptocurrency 'kwatcoin' (https://kwatcoin.org, https://ktcwallet.com) built on its own blockchain technology called the Kwatcoin Blockchain that is gaining so much ground across the world. He is also the founder and president of Wisdom Kwati Foundation, a charity-based foundation in Nigeria with focus on giving children shelter under the Wisdom Kwati Children Village Project.

Money Rule is his second book.

ABOUT THE BOOK

Do you want to earn more but you lack knowledge of how to save the money when it comes? Or you earn money but cannot account for it? Are you an employee who earns monthly pay but lacks financial discipline? This makes you go into debts even before your next paycheque.

Or let's say you run a business that should be bringing you income but each time, you find yourself at the verge of going into financial crisis. Or perhaps you have money but lack knowledge of smart investment models and strategies to work with. This leaves you sceptical about investing your money.

If this is your case, your solution is here.

MONEY RULE is a book that will show you how to make more money, invest it, and build wealth. This book will expose you to seeming money mistakes a lot of people make and show you ways to avert them and live a debt-free life. It is a complete guide for all who want FINANCIAL FREEDOM. Get to know more and see more reviews on https://wisdomkwati.com/moneyrule

MIX
Papier aus verantwortungsvollen Quellen
Paper from responsible sources
FSC® C105338

Printed by Books on Demand GmbH, Norderstedt / Germany